Great Players
in
Alabama Football

Alabama history has its share of great football players

The book is written for those of us who love Alabama Crimson Tide Football. and its great and storied football players. Crimson Tide football supporters cannot wait until the next UA win.

The book is quite simple in that it first tells the story about how the game of football came about in the US; then it describes how Alabama football came into being. Then, we examine the great all-conference and all-American players and other great Alabama players who made the program so successful.

Alabama fans know that in 1892, the University's first football team assembled calling itself the "Thin Red Line." From a bit thin in the ranks, to later becoming the crushing "Crimson Tide," this book gets you to the point that you can look at great Alabama players from over the years and enjoy reading about their outstanding accomplishments.

You will find highlights of great players in Alabama football and be able to read a narrative of each regarding their exceptional prowess, their impact on Alabama football, and their impact on pro football. To stage the reader for future Alabama greatness, we also recap the 2017 championship game and offer unique insights. Now that the loss to Clemson is behind us all, we can move on to the future greatness we always expect from the Crimson Tide.

None of the players highlighted are suggested to be the greatest. They are in this book, which promises to grow over time as *great* Alabama players. There may be a player who is greater or the greatest ever. I leave that to the pundits and the fans. There are hundreds of great Alabama players from 1892 to today, and we look at many who simply stand-out among their peers.

In this book, we find names such as Riley Smith, Harry Gilmer, Bart Starr, Kenny Stabler, AJ McCarron, Joe Namath, Cornelius Bennett, Mark Ingram and others. I can't wait to read this as a finished book. I hope you feel the same way.

You will not be able to put this book down

Brian Kelly

Copyright © January 2017, Brian W. Kelly Editor: Brian P. Kelly
Great Players in Alabama Football Author: Brian W. Kelly

All rights reserved: No part of this book may be reproduced or transmitted in any form, or by any means, electronic or mechanical, including photocopying, recording, scanning, faxing, or by any information storage and retrieval system, without permission from the publisher, LETS GO PUBLISH, in writing.

Disclaimer: Though judicious care was taken throughout the writing and the publication of this work that the information contained herein is accurate, there is no expressed or implied warranty that all information in this book is 100% correct. Therefore, neither LETS GO PUBLISH, nor the author accepts liability for any use of this work.

Trademarks: A number of products and names referenced in this book are trade names and trademarks of their respective companies.

Referenced Material: *Standard Disclaimer: The information in this book has been obtained through personal and third party observations, interviews, and copious research. Where unique information has been provided or extracted from other sources, those sources are acknowledged within the text of the book itself or in the References area in the front matter. Thus, there are no formal footnotes nor is there a bibliography section. Any picture that does not have a source was taken from various sites on the Internet with no credit attached. If resource owners would like credit in the next printing, please email publisher.*

Published by: LETS GO PUBLISH!
Editor in Chief Brian P. Kelly
Email: info@letsgopublish.com
Web site   www.letsgopublish.com

Library of Congress Copyright Information Pending
Book Cover Design by **Michele Thomas;**   **Editor—Brian P. Kelly**

ISBN Information: The International Standard Book Number (ISBN) is a unique machine-readable identification number, which marks any book unmistakably. The ISBN is the clear standard in the book industry. 159 countries and territories are officially ISBN members. The Official ISBN For this book is   **978-0-9982683-9-2**

The price for this work is: **$ 9.99 USD**

10   9   8   7   6   5   4   3   2   1

Release Date: February 2017

Alabama Season Records from 1892 through 2017

Year	Coach	Conference	Record	C-Record
1892	E. B. Beaumont #1	Independent	2-2-0	
1893	Eli Abbott #2	Independent	0-4-0	
1894	Eli Abbott	Independent	3-1-0	
1895	Eli Abbott	SIAA	0-4-0	0-4-0
1896	Otto Wagonhurst #3	SIAA	2-1-0	1-1-0
1897	Allen McCants #4	SIAA	1-0-0	0-0-0
1898	No Season—WW I			
1899	W. A. Martin #5	SIAA	3-1-0	1-0-0
1900	Malcolm Griffin #6	SIAA	2-3-0	1-3-0
1901	M. S. Harvey #7	SIAA	2-1-2	2-1-2
1902	Eli Abbott #8	SIAA	4-4-0	2-4-0
1903	W. B. Blount #9	SIAA	3-4-0	3.4-0
1904	W. B. Blount	SIAA	7-3-0	4-3-0
1905	Jack Leavenworth #10	SIAA	6-4-0	4-4-0
1906	J. W. H. Pollard #11	SIAA	5-1-0	3-1-0
1907	J. W. H. Pollard	SIAA	5-1-2	3-1-2
1908	J. W. H. Pollard	SIAA	6-1-1	1-1-1
1909	J. W. H. Pollard	SIAA	5-1-2	4-1-2
1910	Guy Lowman #12	SIAA	4-4-0	0-4-0
1911	D. V. Graves #13	SIAA	5-2-2	2-2-2
1912	D. V. Graves	SIAA	5-3-1	3-3-1
1913	D. V. Graves	SIAA	6-3-0	4-3-0
1914	D. V. Graves	SIAA	5-4-0	4-3-0
1915	Thomas Kelley #14	SIAA	6-2-0	5-0-0
1916	Thomas Kelley	SIAA	6-3-0	4-3-0
1917	Thomas Kelley	SIAA	5-2-1	3-1-1
1918	B. L. Noojin #15	SIAA	* WWI No games	
1919	Xen C. Scott #16	SIAA	8-1-1	6-1-0
1920	Xen C. Scott	SIAA	10-1-0	6-1-0
1921	Xen C. Scott	SIAA	5-4-2	2-4-2
1922	Xen C. Scott	SoCon	6-3-1	3-2-1
1923	Wallace Wade #17	SoCon	7-2-0	4-1-1
1924	Wallace Wade	SoCon	8-1-0	5-0-0
1925*	Wallace Wade	SoCon	10-0-0	7-0-0
1926*	Wallace Wade	SoCon	9-0-1	8-0-0
1927	Wallace Wade	SoCon	5-4-1	3-4-1
1928	Wallace Wade	SoCon	6-3-0	6-2-0
1929	Wallace Wade	SoCon	6-3-0	4-3-0
1930*	Wallace Wade	SoCon	10-0-0	8-0-0

Year	Coach	Conference	Overall	Conference
1931	Frank Thomas #18	SoCon	9-1-0	7-1-0
1932	Frank Thomas	SoCon	8-2-0	5-2-0
1933	Frank Thomas	SEC	7-1-1	5-0-1
1934*	Frank Thomas	SEC	10-0-0	7-0-0
1935	Frank Thomas	SEC	6-2-1	4-2-0
1936	Frank Thomas	SEC	8-0-1	5-0-1
1937	Frank Thomas	SEC	9-1-0	6-0-0
1938	Frank Thomas	SEC	7-1-1	4-1-1
1939	Frank Thomas	SEC	5-3-1	2-3-1
1940	Frank Thomas	SEC	7-2-0	4-2-0
1941*	Frank Thomas	SEC	9-2-0	5-2-0
1942	Frank Thomas	SEC	8-3-0	4-2-0
1943	No games WW II			
1944	Frank Thomas	SEC	5-2-2	3-1-2
1945	Frank Thomas	SEC	10-0-0	6-0-0
1946	Frank Thomas	SEC	7-4-0	4-3-0
1947	Harold Drew # 19	SEC	8-3-0	5-2-0
1948	Harold Drew	SEC	6-4-1	4-4-1
1949	Harold Drew	SEC	6-3-1	4-3-1
1950	Harold Drew	SEC	9-2-0	6-2-0
1951	Harold Drew	SEC	5-6-0	3-5-0
1952	Harold Drew	SEC	10-2-0	4-2-0
1953	Harold Drew	SEC	6-3-3	4-0-3
1954	Harold Drew	SEC	4-5-2	3-3-2
1955	Jennings Whitworth #20	SEC	0-10-0	0-7-0
1956	Jennings Whitworth	SEC	2-7-1	2-5-0
1957	Jennings Whitworth	SEC	2-7-1	1-6-1
1958	Bear Bryant #21	SEC	5-4-1	3-4-1
1959	Bear Bryant	SEC	7-2-2	4-1-2
1960	Bear Bryant	SEC	8-1-2	5-1-1
1961*	Bear Bryant	SEC	11-0-0	7-0-0
1962	Bear Bryant	SEC	10-1-0	6-1-0
1963	Bear Bryant	SEC	9-2-0	6-2-0
1964*	Bear Bryant	SEC	10-1-0	8-0-0
1965*	Bear Bryant	SEC	9-1-1	6-1-1
1966	Bear Bryant	SEC	11-0-0	6-0-0
1967	Bear Bryant	SEC	8-2-1	5-1-0
1968	Bear Bryant	SEC	8-3-0	4-2-0
1969	Bear Bryant	SEC	6-5-0	2-4-0
1970	Bear Bryant	SEC	6-5-1	3-4-0
1971	Bear Bryant	SEC	11-1-0	7-0-0
1972	Bear Bryant	SEC	10-2-0	7-1-0

Year	Coach	Conference	Record	Conference Record
1973*	Bear Bryant	SEC	11-1-0	8-0-0
1974	Bear Bryant	SEC	11-1-0	6-0-0
1975	Bear Bryant	SEC	11-1-0	6-0-0
1976	Bear Bryant	SEC	9-3-0	5-2-0
1977	Bear Bryant	SEC	11-1-0	7-0-0
1978*	Bear Bryant	SEC	11-1-0	6-0-0
1979*	Bear Bryant	SEC	12-0-0	6-0-0
1980	Bear Bryant	SEC	10-2-0	5-1-0
1981	Bear Bryant	SEC	9-2-1	6-0-0
1982	Bear Bryant	SEC	8-4-0	3-3-0
1983	Ray Perkins #22	SEC	8-4-0	4-2-0
1984	Ray Perkins	SEC	5-6-0	2-4-0
1985	Ray Perkins	SEC	9-2-1	4-1-1
1986	Ray Perkins	SEC	10-3-0	4-2-0
1987	Bill Curry # 23	SEC	7-5-0	4-3-0
1988	Bill Curry	SEC	9-3-0	4-3-0
1989	Bill Curry	SEC	10-2-0	6-1-0
1990	Gene Stallings #24	SEC	7-5-0	5-2-0
1991	Gene Stallings	SEC	11-1-0	6-1-1
1992*	Gene Stallings	SEC	13-0-0	8-0-0
1993	Gene Stallings	SEC	9-3-1 (1-0)	5-2-1 (0)
1994	Gene Stallings	SEC	12-1-0	8-0-0
1995	Gene Stallings	SEC	8-3-0	5-3-0
1996	Gene Stallings	SEC	10-3-0	6-2-0
1997	Mike DuBose #25	SEC	4-7-0	2-6-0
1998	Mike DuBose	SEC	7-5-0	4-4-0
1999	Mike DuBose	SEC	10-3-0	7-1-0
2000	Mike DuBose	SEC	3-8-0	3-5-0
2001	D. Franchione #26	SEC	7-5-0	4-4-0
2002	D. Franchione	SEC	10-3-0	6-2-0
2003	Mike Price #27	SEC	5 months --- No games	
2004	Mike Shula #28	SEC	4-9-0	2-6-0
2005	Mike Shula	SEC	6-6-0	3-5-0
2006	Mike Shula	SEC	10-2-0	6-2-0
2007	Shula Sanctions	SEC	0-2-0	0-2-0
2008	Mike Shula	SEC	6-7-0	2-6-0
2009	Joe Kines #29 Interim	SEC	0-1-0	0-0-0
2007	Nick Saban # 29	SEC	7-6-0	4-4-0
2008	Nick Saban	SEC	12-2-0	8-0-0
2009*	Nick Saban	SEC	14-0-0	8-0-0
2010	Nick Saban	SEC	10-3-0	5-3-0
2011*	Nick Saban	SEC	12-1-0	7-1-0

2012*	Nick Saban	SEC	13-1-0	7-1-0
2013	Nick Saban	SEC	11-2-0	7-1-0
2014	Nick Saban	SEC	12-2-0	7-1-0
2015*	Nick Saban	SEC	14-1-0	7-1-0
2016	Nick Saban	SEC	14-1-0	8-0-0

- = National Championships

Total Wins   879
Total Losses   327
Total Ties   43   Prior to Overtime Rules
Stats from   1892   Through December 2016

Alabama Coaches Over the Years

Year	Coach	
1892	E. B. Beaumont	#1
1893	Eli Abbott	#2
1896	Otto Wagonhurst	#3
1897	Allen McCants	#4
1899	W. A. Martin	#5
1900	Malcolm Griffin	#6
1901	M. S. Harvey	#7
1902	Eli Abbott	#8 & #2
1903	W. B. Blount	#9
1905	Jack Leavenworth	#10
1906	J. W. H. Pollard	#11
1910	Guy Lowman	#12
1911	D. V. Graves	#13
1915	Thomas Kelley	#14
1918	B. L. Noojin	#15
1919	Xen C. Scott	#16
1923	Wallace Wade	#17
1931	Frank Thomas	#18
1947	Harold Drew	#19
1955	Jennings Whitworth	#20
1958	Paul "Bear" Bryant	#21
1982	Ray Perkins	#22
1983	Bill Curry	#23
1984	Gene Stallings	#24
1985	Mike DuBose	#25
1986	D. Franchione	#26
1987	Mike Price	#27
1988	Mike Shula	#28
1989	Joe Kines Interim	#29
2007	Nick Saban	#30

Those are the seasons and the numbers, folks!

LETS GO
PUBLISH!

Dedication

As a person with a big family on my side and on my wife's side. I am pleased to dedicate this book as I have with others to my wonderful family.

Thank you to all of the Piotroski's—(Arline & Stanley Sr.), (Marty & Cathy), (Stan, Archie & Carol), (Sue & Mitch), and all their progeny—for support in all of my publishing efforts.

Wily Ky Eyeley, my sage niece, offers most appreciated advice continually.

And, of course the Kelly's (Ed & Irene) and my brothers and sisters, from my older brother Ed who continually helped me go for it—even when it seemed hopeless, to all of my other brothers and sisters – (Nancy & Jim), & the Twins (Mary + Bill) & (Joe + Diane), for staying with me in support as I tried to write the world's best something about something.

I really appreciate my entire family's help in everything I do. My wife Pat is phenomenal as are my children, Brian, Michael and Katie.

My family and friends make life easier for me in writing books and everything else. Thank you all—all the people I love the most in life for always being in my corner.

Thank you for helping me. God bless you!

Acknowledgments:

I appreciate all the help that I received in putting this book together, along with the 66 other books from the past.

My printed acknowledgments were once so large that book readers needed to navigate too many pages to get to page one of the text. To permit me more flexibility, I put my acknowledgment list online at www.letsgopublish.com. The list of acknowledgments continues to grow. Believe it or not, it once cost about a dollar more to print each book.

Thank you all on the big list in the sky and God bless you all for your help.

Please check out www.letsgopublish.com to read the latest version of my heartfelt acknowledgments updated for this book. Thank you all!

Preface:

We all know that Paul 'Bear' Bryant was one of college football's most legendary coaches. As a head coach at Maryland, Kentucky, Texas A&M, and Alabama, Bryant impacted the lives of many and left a lasting legacy on the sport and the schools where he worked. He had a short life filled by leading the greatest football teams of all times. He always offered his thoughts about the notion of football and the strategies of many who he competed against. The Bear took prisoners but he released them right after the games.

As a student and an athlete at Alabama, Bear Bryant represented all the greats who did not get his fame – Wallace Wade, and Frank Thomas, and Gene Stallings especially, He knew how to win in football and in life: "If you want to walk the heavenly streets of gold, you gotta know the password, 'Roll, Tide, Roll' "—Bear Bryant.

In a book titled, Great Moments in Alabama Football, which is still in process and will be much more comprehensive than this and larger in terms of # of pages, I dedicated a chapter to the life of Bear Bryant. He is so much a part of the fabric of the University of Alabama's sports programs, especially football. I eulogized the Bear in this chapter and I will share with you some words I sent to my good friends and family as I was writing the book. I titled the email "I think Bear Bryant and God are buddies. Do you agree?" I ended it with the following::

""Rest in Peace Dear Coach Paul W. "Bear" Bryant. You are a real man among men and God made you so that you could build your legacy of goodness and greatness so that all can know it is good to be good; it is great to be great; it is the greatest notion to be the best. Better than best. Perhaps it is as good as it gets to know that you are the best and while alive, you are to humbly just keep on winning. Just keep winning! We all know that Bear Bryant hated losses but he understood and respected the dignity of showing true humility in the face of defeat. God also hates losses-especially lost souls. With all due respect, Lord, you and Bear Bryant have a lot in common!"

One of my good friends who responded to my note is Jack Lammers, a one-time starting quarterback at Villanova. Jack is just about in his eighties now but you would never know it. An athlete in his forties would be proud to look as well as Jack carries himself. Jack loves football everywhere. He recalled fondly and with respect meeting up with Bear Bryant as a player before the Bear took over the Alabama Program. I think you will enjoy his words. It is representative of the world of football through an opponent's eyes. Enjoy:

"Brian,
In my senior year we played against The Bear's Texas A&M team down in College Station. They were the Junction Boys and I am sure that you saw that term in your research. Among them was John David Crowe who won the Heisman that year. They were the SW Conference champs and we played them a pretty good game. We had them tied at the half but they finally won 19-6. In those days of limited substitution, The Bear just substituted eleven new players every five minutes and they wore us down.
Jack"

Can't you sense the respect and the frustration in Jack's words? It is both real and humorous if, of course, you were not playing *against* a Bear-coached team.

Even though this footnote on the Junction boys is not about Alabama per se., it is about Bear Bryant. Texas A&M University had hired Bear Bryant as its head football coach in 1954, replacing former coach Ray George. Bryant arrived in College Station on February 8, 1954, and his first correct supposition was that the team was weak. He began cleaning house. He did not think the training program had been effective and he believed the players were not coached well.

He decided that the players needed some remedial treatment for their conditioning and their attitudes about winning He chose a camp site away from the distractions on campus in the small Hill Country town of Junction, where Texas A&M owned more than enough property.

Texas often has periods of drought and when camp began on September 1, it was one of the worst drought and heat wave combinations in history. It was four years old and would last another two years after the 10-day camp was completed. A number of days during the camp were over 100 degrees F.

Bear ran the team before dawn until the day was done with meetings in the evening until 11:00 pm. It was too much for many Each day fewer and fewer showed up for practice. The objective was to toughen up the players. One of the Junction Boys, future NFL coach Jack Pardee, would later say in an interview that it was not unheard of for players to sweat away 10% of their body weight. Just about 30 of those who made the Junction trip were with the team when A & M

The ordeal has achieved legendary status. It was the subject of a 2001 book "The Junction Boys" by Jim Dent. There was also a television movie produced by ESPN that had Tom Berenger playing Coach Bryant. Despite the grueling camp, the team recorded a 1-9 record in 1954. They had been toughened but even Bear could not teach talent. He had to accelerate his recruiting engine to begin to win.

My friend Jack Lammers from Villanova played well against these guys in 1956. A&M was dominant in 1956. The crew from camp were tougher than nails, though only eight Junction players were still on this team that won the title. Bryant led the tea in 1956 to a 9-0-1 record. A&M was to be the SWC nominee in the Cotton Bowl but two-year old recruiting violations from basketball caused the NCAA to take away the team's right to play. Perhaps Bear would have had a championship with the Aggies before Alabama.

There is a reason for everything in life.

"Crimson tide" is a term coined by an Alabama reporter to describe the University of Alabama football team's brilliant defense against rival Auburn during a 1907 football game played in a "sea of red mud." The term stuck and is, to this day, the nickname of the University of Alabama football team.

On October 8, 1930, sports writer Everett Strupper of the Atlanta Journal wrote a story of the Alabama-Mississippi game that he had witnessed in Tuscaloosa four days earlier. Strupper wrote:

"That Alabama team of 1930 is a typical Wade machine, powerful, big, tough, fast, aggressive, well-schooled in fundamentals, and the best blocking team for this early in the season that I have ever seen.

When those big brutes hit you I mean you go down and stay down, often for an additional two minutes.

"Coach [Wallace] Wade started his second team that was plenty big and they went right to their knitting scoring a touchdown in the first quarter against one of the best fighting small lines that I have seen. For Ole Miss was truly battling the big boys for every inch of ground.

"At the end of the quarter, the earth started to tremble, there was a distant rumble that continued to grow. Some excited fan in the stands bellowed, 'Hold your horses, the elephants are coming,' and out stamped this Alabama varsity.

Wade's way was to use the second team to soften the other team. The real elephants however, were only for show.

"It was the first time that I had seen it and the size of the entire eleven nearly knocked me cold, men that I had seen play last year looking like they had nearly doubled in size."

Strupper and other writers continued to refer to the Alabama linemen as "Red Elephants," the color referring to the crimson jerseys. Thus today's elephant mascot for the Tide, is known as Big Al and Al is an elephant. But, Why?

Throughout the 1940s, for instance, the University kept a live elephant mascot named "Alamite" that was a regular sight on game days, and it would carry the year's Homecoming queen onto the field every year prior to kickoff at the Homecoming game.

In the early 1960s, Melford Espey, Jr., then a student, was the first to wear an elephant head costume to portray the Crimson Tide's unofficial mascot. The mascot known as "Big Al" today was the brainchild of

University of Alabama student Walt Tart in 1979 as he was working with Ann Paige on homecoming festivities.

Big Al appeared officially in the 1980 Sugar Bowl in which Alabama won handily 24-7. Big Al helped launch the 12-0 Crimson Tide as another of Bear Bryant's undefeated, untied, national champions.

Big Al celebrated his first year with Bear Bryant's 300th win against the Kentucky Wildcats and a victory against the Baylor Bears in the 1981 Cotton Bowl. Big Al has been part of the Alabama scene ever since.

Alabama built its first version of Bryant-Denny Stadium in the 1920's. It opened in 1929 and was originally named Denny Stadium in honor of George H. Denny. Today, for every home game, every Alabama player walks down the tunnel right before every home game. You will see in this book in the chapters about the most recent seasons, the coach shown in a photo with his football team right behind him waiting to take the field. It is the most exciting part of the pre-game—and then comes the action.

Before the festivities begin for the game, it is fun to visit a few spots on campus Of course all 101,821 Bryant-Denny Stadium fans cannot be in the same place at the same time before the game but they sure try. On the opposite side of Bryant-Denny Stadium from The QUAD is an area known as 'The Strip'.

This stretch of road consists of a few bars, restaurants, and retail shops. You can party on the patio of the Houndstooth Sports Bar, catch some live music at The Jupiter, purchase all the Crimson Tide apparel you'll need at the Alabama Bookstore and make sure to stop by Galette's and try their original drink, The Yellowhammer. One of the most popular pre-and post-game drinks in town!

On the way to the game, fans and players take on the Walk of Champions. The Walk of Champions begins approximately 2 hours and 15 minutes prior to kickoff. The team is dropped off in the team buses on the north side of the stadium at University Boulevard and proceeds through the Walk of Champions into the stadium. It is a grand experience.

Another major UA tradition is the Elephant Stomp. 4. It is a great name for what Alabama likes to think of as an exciting Million Dollar Band pep rally! The fun of the Stomp begins on the steps of the Gorgas Library and it ends with a march to the stadium. The band begins one hour before kickoff but the drum line begins two hours prior to kickoff. It gets everybody in the spirit.

Today, the *Crimson Tide* as noted above are joined in the campus pre-game festivities to celebrate the goodness of football to the university. They join with members of the student body, faculty population, alumni, and fans to get the team into a mood for winning the day's game.

Fans are swept in by the stories, and the tradition, and the winning ways of the University of Alabama. This book reenacts many of the same emotions game and will remind all the Alabama faithful about why they are Alabama faithful.

Under its charter, the school is officially the University of Alabama and has been educating young minds since back in the 1820's. The football program began in 1892 and was very successful from the

"Cadets" first moment on the QUAD Field. It took a few years before the Crimson White became the Crimson Tide in 1907.

Another new book by Brian Kelly, about to be released, which highlights the <u>Great Moments in Alabama Football</u> is one of the items that is available all 52 weeks and in fact all 365 days each year. It is about to be available and it will add to your overall Notre Dame football experience. It actually is a superset of this book. Once you get this book, it is yours forever unless, of course you give it away to one of the many who will be in awe.

Whether you get to the festivities and the great games on campus or not, reading about it all in this nearly 600-page book brings the glory of Alabama football right to your bookshelf, your pocket, or right to your hands. Reading this book is like reliving the last game, the last football season, and / or all the seasons before last season without ever having to get on or off a plane.

Back to this book

Opening its first story at the very beginning of Football as a sport in America, this book goes through Alabama's first team, through the great players in the school's history and ends with the CFP Championship game of January 2017.

This book is written for those of us who love Alabama University (AU) Football. This book is all about the great players in Alabama Football and as noted, a little bit more. The Book purposely stops every now and then, and takes the reader on an in-line excursion which looks at great quarterbacks, defensive and offensive linemen, running backs, and receivers. You'll read about the likes of John Hannah, Bart Starr, Cornelius Bennett, Joe Namath, AJ McCarran, Ozzie Newsome, Derrick Thomas, Kenny Stabler, and other Alabama greats.

I predict that you will not be able to put this book down

You are going to love this book because it is the perfect quick read for anybody who loves the University of Alabama and Alabama Football and wants to know more about one of the most revered athletic program of all time.

Few sports books are a must-read but Brian Kelly's <u>Great Players in Alabama Football</u> will quickly appear at the top of Americ'as most enjoyable must-read books about sports. Enjoy!

Who is Brian W. Kelly?

Brian W. Kelly is one of the leading authors in America with this, his 98th published book. Brian is an outspoken and eloquent expert on a variety of topics and he has also written several hundred articles on topics of deep interest to Americans.

Most of Brian's early works involved high technology. Later, he wrote a number of patriotic books and most recently he has been writing human interest books such as <u>The Wine Diet</u> and <u>Thank you, IBM</u>. This is his fourth major sports book. Last year he actually wrote three children's books. He enjoyed writing the children's books almost as much as everybody enjoyed reading them. His books are always well received.

Brian Kelly's books are highlighted at www.letsgopublish.com. They are for sale at Amazon and Kindle, and most can be viewed by linking to amazon.com/author/brianwkelly.

Sincerely,

Brian P. Kelly, Editor in Chief
I am Brian Kelly's eldest son

Table of Contents

Chapter 1 Introduction to the Book 1

Chapter 2 Alabama's First Football Team 11

Chapter 3 The Evolution of Modern American Football 23

Chapter 4 Perspective on the Great Players in Alabama Football 43

Chapter 5 Great Alabama Quarterbacks 47

Chapter 6 Great Alabama Receivers 65

Chapter 7 Great Alabama Defenders 79

Chapter 8 Great Alabama Running Backs 91

Chapter 9 Great Alabama Offensive Linemen 101

Chapter 10 Intro to 2016 Season & CFP Championship Game 113

Other books by Brian Kelly: (amazon.com, and Kindle) 126

About the Author

Brian Kelly retired as an Assistant Professor in the Business Information Technology (BIT) Program at Marywood University, where he also served as the IBM i and Midrange Systems Technical Advisor to the IT Faculty. Kelly designed, developed, and taught many college and professional courses. He continues as a contributing technical editor to a number of technical industry magazines, including "The Four Hundred" and "Four Hundred Guru," published by IT Jungle.

Kelly is a former IBM Senior Systems Engineer. His specialty was problem solving for customers as well as implementing advanced operating systems and software on his client's machines. Brian is the author of 98 books and hundreds of magazine articles. He has been a frequent speaker at technical conferences throughout the United States.

Brian was a candidate for the US Congress from Pennsylvania in 2010 and he ran for Mayor in his home town in 2015. He loves Alabama Football and thoroughly enjoyed writing this book about Alabama football's great moments.

Chapter 1 Introduction to the Book

Alabama celebrates its many national college football championships in its 125th year.

Nick Saban, Immortal Alabama Coach "Post Bear" Leading the Crimson Tide

In 2017, Alabama celebrates its 125th year. As part of the celebration, the University would be pleased for you to visit its athletic website that honors all Crimson Tide Sports. I promise that if AU chooses to create a new web site commemorating this great moment in its football history of 125 years in 2017, I will create a new version of this book to provide you all with the link and I will update the Kindle version so it can be downloaded immediately. Thank you for reading this book. I know you will love it as you love the Alabama Crimson Tide.

This book is proud to celebrate Alabama University Football; its founding; its struggles; its greatness; and its long-lasting impact on American life. People like me, who love the greatness of Alabama University, will love this book. Alabama haters will want their own copy of just for additional ammo (facts). Yet, it won't help them! Hah!

We begin the rest of the Alabama Football Story in Chapter 2 with the founding of the institution and we continue in subsequent chapters right into the founding of the football program in 1892.

In defining the format of the book, we chose to use a timetable that is based on a historical chronology. Within this framework, we discuss the great moments in Alabama Football History, and there are many great moments. No book can claim to be able to capture them all, as it would be a never-ending story, but we sure try.

Any former coach or player from Alabama can attest to the fact that despite all the great coaches and players perhaps no Alabama jerseys could be retired because with all of the history of this great program, there would be no numbers left.

I like to use this idea to help promulgate the notion that nobody can write a full book about Alabama Football History that is all inclusive, because even if it can be written, it would be too big to ever be read. I hoped this book would come in at a little over 200 pages, but if it had, you would not have liked it. Read what you can in this book when you can. If you love Alabama, it will surely be a fun experience.

I capture all the great moments in this book. OK, I get most of them! If I missed any and you tell me, then we'll do a second edition and a third and a fourth but we'll get it right. The great moments naturally include a lot of great people, including players and the 29 great coaches that over time would make or break the University of Alabama

If Alabama were ever to break because of any coach, as some believe it has at times, (but the UA legacy proves these were only bends, not breaks) simply because it is Alabama U, the University not only would continue from any issue coming its way. it will always continue. History proves that. Alabama has a he** of a lot of moxie as an institution. Roll Tide on that for sure.

After 29 mostly great coaches and as non-fans actually believe -- a zillion national championships, UA has been able to again become the most respected program of its peers and it is also now the most feared and the most respected college football team of the modern era. If you don't believe that, then you are simply not paying attention.

Ask any coach in 2017, which team would you prefer not to play, and the answer would not be anything other than Alabama U. That is the reality of having a winning record and a coach who can win anywhere!

Alabama has been able to survive a number of coaches who could not survive themselves, while the university and the football program have both grown in acceptance and popularity.

We all as individuals and as honest institutions, such as Alabama do our best in life and sometimes it is just enough. Sometimes it is just not enough. Even if we survive and become more than OK, detractors may suggest our success is not enough. I disagree. Let the naysayers say "nay," and go away! Who can deny Alabama is the greatest football team that ever lived. I bet Knute Rockne would give today's coach Nick Sabin a fine "High Five."

Let me please assure you that I have done my best to portray an accurate depiction of Alabama Football History, displayed in a properly summarized format so that none of us are reading this book forever. There are a ton of great stories for sure. More importantly, none of us should need to search further than this book for the truth about many of the depictions in this book.

I worried from the inception of this project about how I could reduce Alabama Football to a book. I can't! Nobody can! But we can do something close to satisfying what needs to be said about this outstanding football program, fully supported by the institution as well as the whole state of Alabama.

In fact I can, and I have done so in this book. We can deliver an understanding of Alabama Football and all of its years without talking about the mice that ate the cheese in the men's locker room in game X of season Y. Yes, indeed. I am pleased that I have achieved this objective in this book.

Who thinks that in 2017, there is a better team in college football than Alabama? Pardon my French but only an idiot!

Alabama has its own legacy as do many great college programs but an honest look says Alabama is so unusual, it is undeniably the greatest program ever in college football. It does not matter from which university you gained your alma mater. If you like Football and you like honesty and you like winning, Alabama is the only good bet in town.

The secret in writing this book has been to know that there is always more. My job has been to show things that are known already in encyclopedias, and the vast resources of the Internet. I did not have to personally speak with Mr. Bryant or Mr. Stallings, or Mr. Saban to get the truth about what was happening in their lives or the football time-period in which they exceled. It shows in their records.

Alabama won lots of games with teams on offense and defense better than any others

Alabama has no revered history of groups of players such as the *four horsemen* of Notre Dame gaining recognition above and beyond the program and the team. Alabama's coaches over the years especially Bear Bryant and now Nick Saban have taken great athletes, who had no clue how far they could go, without fanfare, and these great coaches turned them into great players.

The players for their own reason did not group together into the four horsemen or the five oxes or the three birds or anything like that as their mission was to play great for the University of Alabama and they gained their reputations from doing exactly that.

I have done no magic in this book and I know it well, But nobody else has ever done what I have done with a project such as this. I have taken the well-known Alabama football history of our times and I have made it both readable and exciting, even without including every phrase, paraphrase, paragraph, sentence, conjunctive verb, or otherwise forgotten notion that may have been included in somebody else's description of events.

If this book were written to be 75,000 pages, I still could not have included everything. But, then again, I knew I was not writing a tax code for the US. Who reads the tax code anyway?

My job was to bring this work about UA great moments together, and to show enough to the reader to make the journey through the beginning of football through Coach Saban's last win much easier to make than otherwise it could have ever been. As I read and reread this book myself, I do believe I achieved that objective.

What reader wants to do the research in order to be fulfilled about Alabama football history other than me? This book makes UA history and its great moments in football history both exciting and real. Of course, it is also much easier than if the reader had to look up all this great stuff by himself. It brings the Crimson Tide and Crimson Tide football to life for the reader.

Instead of lots of work, we can just sit in our easy chairs or lounges at the pool or beach and we can learn and enjoy and enjoy and learn about a football team and a university that we have come to love. Along the way, every now and then, we'll probably fall asleep with a smile on our faces, and we'll dream about a fine story starring "the Bear" "AJ McCarren," "Kenny Stabler, "Joe Namath", "Gene Stallings," Xen C. Scott, or Nick Saban himself!

How did I do it? How did I make this book inclusive and yet not exhaustive or exhausting?

I started right at the beginning of the football era, while football was being invented, and the rules were being formed by the greats of the day. Then, I began to write about things as they were happening back then. I moved the book chapter by chapter through the beginning of the University of Alabama; the beginning of football; and then the beginning of Alabama Football. I made sure that I got the essence and that the tales were not boring.

I took the flow of the book through periods in which student athletes were coaching football at Alabama. I took it to eras in which coaches did not last much more than a year while better coaches lasted two to four years. Then, before I knew it I was sneaking up on the decades in which more coaches made an impact in more years than in the beginning through the 1920's. I then took the flow of the book to the era of the great Wallace Wade and Frank Thomas

Then I moved to Bear Bryant and Gene Stallings and I went through each and every one of the thirty University of Alabama football coaches in just enough measure so that we all would know their mission and their results. I made sure that we captured their best stories.

Eventually, as the flow took us through twenty-nine coaches, in 2007, we got to examine a thirtieth coach. That's when Coach Nick Saban was hired by the university. Then, I examined and wrote all about the Nick Saban era, through 2017 and into the next year with the championship game. As I am reviewing Chapter 1 again, making sure I did all I said I would, I find that I have completed the University of Alabama story and the Alabama football story so you can now fill your leisure time with smiles and wonderment. Don't you dare put this book down!

I thought you would like this print by Larry Pitts. Would you not like to have such a print in your rec room? This and other great Larry Pitts Alabama Prints are available at:
http://www.redelephants.com/acatalog/Alabama_Prints_By_Artist_Larry_Pitts_.html

This is a print Larry Pitts did with all the National Champion coaches at Alabama, in a poker game. They are left from right, Gene Stallings, Nick Saban, Frank Thomas, Wallace Wade, and of course, Bear Bryant.

Even if you choose never to take a break while reading this book, I get the whole teaching job done in something just less than 600 pages of the most enjoyable content you will ever read. It's all about Alabama Football, Who could ask for more!

Coach Saban extended the great Alabama coaching era right to today. Coach Nick Saban, not the least of the greats for sure, is also not the last. I see the current coach as he directs this team, to continue to become the best of the best. And the hallowed immortals will not be able to deny Coach Saban his immortality claim. Nor would they want to do so. Let Nick Saban live long and prosper!

Using this format of *enough told* to get the story told, in the rest of the chapters in this book, we examine every football season from the first in 1892 to the last, which as of today is the Nick Saban Era's 2016 season with his four Alabama National Championships and fifth overall championship making up his great record.

Within each season, as depicted in the book, we highlight its great moments but we also do one thing that makes this book useful as a reference document about all of the Alabama Football Teams of the past. We chronicle each and every game in text summary form. Some games are portrayed with great detail after the summation because of their historical significance or simply to tell a great story about a great game; great coach; great player; or sometimes even a great opponent.

Nonetheless, all games are listed and chronicled from 1992. You will absolutely love this book from page 1 to the end. Each time I read it now that it is built, I enjoy it even more.

In this book, we tell you the season, the opponent, the venue (home or away), and of course we tell you the outcome with a score that is easy to find. And, then to make it even easier to analyze and browse for specifics, we designate each win or loss with a big W or a big L so that it stands out in the text.

The University of Alabama is proud of its history and its founding by the state legislature and its first president Alva Woods. And, of course Alabama is very proud of its football program, and its legacy.

The Crimson Tide was, is and will continue to be a great university first, and a great home for the greatest football teams that God has ever created or will create.

Thanks for choosing to take this fun ride with us through Alabama Football History. The great moments noted in this book are simply great! You'll love them!

Chapter 2 Alabama's First Football Team

Alabama

Alabama Cadets First Football Team – 1892

1892: Over 70 years from the founding

Alabama Lunches its first football team

They say that Alabama football began with a game in Birmingham on a Friday afternoon in November of 1892. But, there was more to the story than just showing up for the game.

One of my favorite sayings in life is that "nothing worth having in life is easy." Even something as simple as forming a football team at a premiere university that had little knowledge or inclination of the game. Sometimes, a little help from the outside is all that is needed to start a tide rolling.

It happens that for the University of Alabama, all the historical logs suggest it was not the President or Board of Directors or an Athletic Director or a local sports club that got the Tide rolling for Alabama Football. No, it was none of those. It was a law student William G. Little of Livingston, Alabama.

He had learned how to play American football as it was evolving in the US, while he was attending prep school in Andover, Massachusetts. Little was smitten by the game and he soon began teaching the sport to fellow Alabama students in early 1892.

For full context, there was no football at Alabama in 1891. From then to now, it was a rarity when there was no football season for the University of Alabama. Only an event such as a poor administrative decision or a World War would stop Alabama's great football teams from playing.

Later that year (1892), thanks to Little and a dedicated crew of fellow football lovers, the school put together an official team of 19 players, Across the country, more and more colleges and universities were beginning to officially get on board with American football, so this was not exactly new but it sure was groundbreaking for the University.

It is said that when Little arrived, he was "carrying his uniform and a great bag of enthusiasm for the game in 1892." A number of students joined in with him when the season began in October, 1892 after a lot of time spent on formative activities. There is an account in the Crimson White Student Paper from Nov. 25, 1926 that chronicles this trailblazing experience.

Little became the captain of the fledgling group and E. B. Beaumont was the first official head coach. The Collegiate newspaper remarked that Beaumont was fired at season end because he knew too little about the game.

The history for this time in football history is not perfect but it is known that among others on the team was William B. Bankhead, future U.S. Speaker of the House, and Bibb Graves, future governor of Alabama. This first team was referred to as the "Cadets", the "Crimson White", or simply as "the varsity. The guys on this team had one heck of a love for the game.

The 1892 Alabama Cadets football team represented the University of Alabama in the 1892 college football season. The Crimson Tide moniker had not yet been applied. The team was led by their head coach E. B. Beaumont and played their home games at Lakeview Park in Birmingham, Alabama.

Alabama's First Football Coach E. B. Beaumont

In what was the inaugural season of Alabama football, the team finished with a record of two wins and two losses (2–2). For this point values were different from those used in contemporary games. In 1892, for example, a touchdown was worth four points, a field goal was worth five points and an extra point was worth two points

Back to William Little of Livingston, Alabama. He is credited with being responsible for the introduction of football at the university. After playing the game in 1891 while in attendance at a northern prep school, he played a huge role in establishing the first team for the 1892 season.

The first game in Alabama football history was played on November 11, 1892, against Birmingham High School and was won by the Cadets 56–0. They then split a pair of games with the Birmingham Athletic Club, and closed out the season with a 32–22 loss in the first Iron Bowl against Auburn on February 22, 1893. After the season, Beaumont was fired as head coach and replaced by Eli Abbott for the 1893 season.

After Beaumont's departure, William G. Little continued the training of the team until Abbott was formally brought-in to serve as head coach for the 1893 season.

In early newspaper accounts of Alabama football, the team was often simply listed as the "varsity" or the "Crimson White" after the school colors.

The first nickname to become popular and used by headline writers was the "Thin Red Line." The nickname was used until 1906.

Folklore is sometimes lore but it sometimes is mixed with all the facts needed. The name "Crimson Tide" is supposed to have first been used by Hugh Roberts, former sports editor of the Birmingham Age-Herald. He used "Crimson Tide" to describe an Alabama-Auburn game played in Birmingham in 1907.

This ironically was the last football contest between the two schools until 1948 when the series was resumed. The 1907 game was played in a sea of mud and Auburn was a heavy favorite to win.

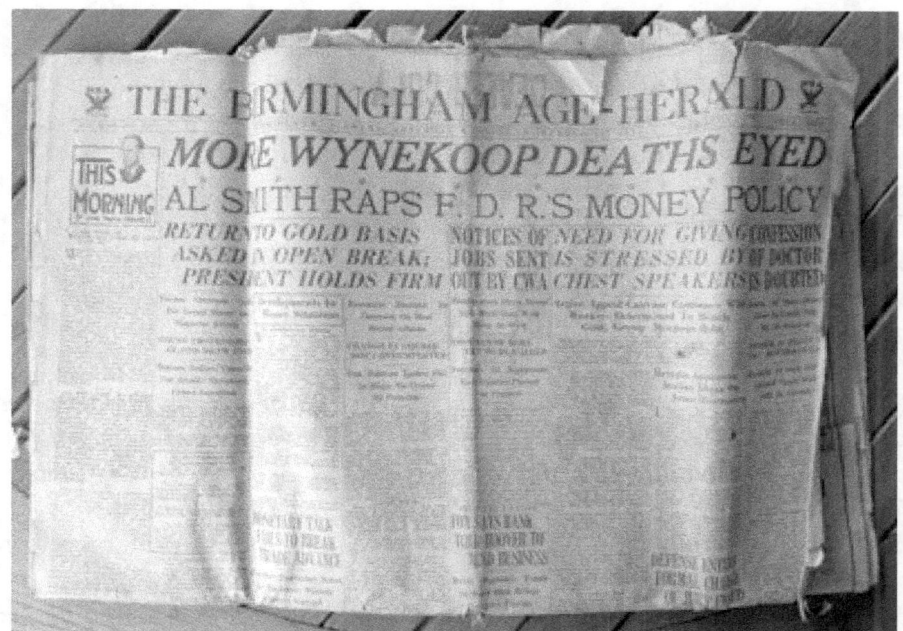
Birmingham Age Herald Front Page Circa 1933 (Last Edition in 1950)

But, evidently, the "Thin Red Line" played a great game in the red mud and held Auburn to a 6-6 tie, thus gaining the name "Crimson Tide." Zipp Newman, former sports editor of the Birmingham News, is credited with popularizing the name more than any other writer. Everything that is has a beginning and often beginnings recounted from times past are a little murky if not downright muddy.

In 1930, Everett Strupper of the Atlanta Journal described the team as 'elephants' when they stomped over Ole Miss, and the mascot stuck. This is a fitting sized animal to describe a program with a successful history of mammoth proportions.

The football team didn't garner national acclaim until a game in Philadelphia in 1922, where Alabama defeated the University of Pennsylvania 9-7. Wallace Wade became the coach the following season. The University of Pennsylvania was an early football powerhouse and had enjoyed prominence trouncing the better teams of the day, including Notre Dame. ai

http://bryantmuseum.com/page.asp?ID=19

The Bryant Web Site offers this account of the early goings:

"Alabama's first game was played in Birmingham on Friday afternoon, Nov. 11, 1892, at the old Lakeview Park. Opposition was furnished by a picked team from Professor Taylor's school and Birmingham high schools, with Alabama winning, 56-0. Early teams were a bit tougher than current squads, it seems, as the following afternoon Alabama played the Birmingham Athletic Club, losing 5-4 when Ross, of B.A.C., kicked a 65-yard field goal. Impossible though it may seem, this field goal was listed as a collegiate record at one time and Birmingham papers of the day featured its distance in writeups of the game.

"The gridiron sport rapidly caught the students' fancy and the game became a favorite with University athletes. In 1896 the University's board of trustees passed a rule forbidding athletic teams from traveling off the campus. The following season only one game was played and in 1898 football was abandoned at Alabama. Student opposition to the ruling was so strong that the trustees lifted the travel ban and football was resumed in 1899, to continue without interruption until the First World War forced cancellation of the 1918 games.

"Alabama first gained national recognition in 1922 when the University of Pennsylvania [a well-known major powerhouse at the time] was defeated, 9-7, in Philadelphia. The following season Wallace Wade became head coach and in 1925 led the Crimson Tide to its first undefeated and untied season and its first Rose Bowl invitation. On Jan. 1, 1926, an unheralded, underrated team from Tuscaloosa came from behind to upset Washington, 20-19, in the Rose Bowl and established a precedent of colorful play that Crimson Tide teams have continued to uphold."

Additional Crimson Tide information can be found at https://en.wikipedia.org/wiki/Alabama_Crimson_Tide_football

Crimson Tide football through the years

The Alabama Crimson Tide football team represents the University of Alabama (aka Alabama, UA, or 'Bama) in the sport of American football. Alabama today competes in the Football Bowl

Subdivision (FBS) of the National Collegiate Athletic Association (NCAA) and the Western Division of the Southeastern Conference (SEC). Currently coached by Nick Saban, UA is one of the most storied and decorated football programs in NCAA history.

Having begun play about 125 years ago in 1892, the program boasts of 16 national championships. These have been coming for a long time—over and over and over again...and they are still coming today.

Ironically, as good as Alabama's program has been since its first Championship in 1925, and despite numerous other national and conference championships, it was not until 2009 that an Alabama player received a Heisman Trophy. It was running back Mark Ingram. He became the university's first winner. In 2015, Derrick Henry became the university's second Heisman winner.

When the 2015 season was completed, Alabama had amassed 864 official victories in NCAA Division I and for those counting at home folks, there were an additional 21 victories that were vacated and another 8 victories and 1 tie were forfeited for various reasons over the years.

The Crimson Tide today plays its home games at Bryant–Denny Stadium, located on its campus in Tuscaloosa, Alabama. It is a huge stadium. With a capacity of 101,821, Bryant-Denny Stadium is the 8th largest non-racing stadium in the world and the seventh largest stadium in the United States.

Head Football Coaches

Since 1892 when the program was formed and 1893, when the first game was played, Alabama has played 122 seasons with 30 head coaches. This includes a 1918 coach in a season in which no games were played and a temporary coach who coached one bowl game after his predecessor was fired.

Like all teams of the era save a few from the East, football, in the early years, was not such an easy college sport in which to form a competitive program.

Soon after beginning of play and after a shutdown of the 1898 season due to a ban on away games. The "Crimson Tide" picked up its cherished nickname after the 1907 season. Overall, UA has played more than 1,200 games in their 125 seasons.

In that time, 12 coaches have led the Crimson Tide in postseason bowl games: Wallace Wade, Frank Thomas, Harold D. "Red" Drew, Bear Bryant, Ray Perkins, Bill Curry, Gene Stallings, Mike DuBose, Dennis Franchione, Mike Shula, Joe Kines, and Nick Saban. Eight of those coaches also won conference championships: Wade, Thomas, Drew, Bryant, Curry, Stallings, DuBose, and Saban. During their tenures, Wade, Thomas, Bryant, Stallings, and Saban all won national championships, totaling 16 with the Crimson Tide.

Of the 30 different head coaches who have led the Crimson Tide, Wade, Thomas, Bryant, and Stallings have been inducted into the College Football Hall of Fame. The current head coach is Nick Saban. Saban was hired in January 2007, and he fits the Alabama tradition like a glove. With the 2015 Championship season in the bag, and a 14-1 record in the 2016 season, Saban has amassed 120 victories which includes the great SEC Championship game and the 2016 Peach Bowl.

Alabama National Championships

Alabama is generally credited with 16 national championships though not all have been of the consensus variety. Most universities today give themselves the benefit of the doubt when there is doubt on a championship in a given year.

National Championships before the CFP bowls were hotly contested. National championships in NCAA FBS college football are debated but the NCAA does not officially award the championship. However, it does provide lists of championships awarded by organizations that it does recognizes.

There is an official NCAA 2009 Division I Football Records Book, and this states that: "During the last 138 years, there have been more than 30 selectors of national champions using polls, historical research and mathematical rating systems. Beginning in 1936, the Associated Press (AP) began the best-known and most widely circulated poll of sportswriters and broadcasters. Before 1936, national champions were determined by historical research and retroactive ratings and polls.

The criteria for being included in this historical list of poll selectors is that the poll be national in scope, either through distribution in newspaper, television, radio and/or computer online.

Since World War II, Alabama only claims national championships awarded by the final AP Poll or the final Coaches' Poll. This policy is consistent with other FBS football programs with numerous national title claims, including Notre Dame, USC, and Oklahoma.

All national championships claimed by the University of Alabama were published in nationally syndicated newspapers and magazines, and each of the national championship selectors, and are cited in the Official 2010 NCAA FBS Record Book.

In addition to the championships claimed by the university, the NCAA has listed Alabama as receiving a championship for the 1945, 1966, 1975, and 1977 college football seasons.

In Alabama's own 1982 media guide, the last for Coach Bryant, 1934 is listed as the only national championship before Coach Bryant in a small footnote about the school's SEC history.

In the 1980s, Alabama's Sports Information Director Wayne Atcheson began to recognize five pre-Bryant national championship teams (1925, 1926, 1930, 1934, 1941). He added them to the University's Football Media Guide.

Atcheson said that he made the effort in the context of disputed titles being claimed by other schools, and "to make Alabama football look the best it could look" to compete with the other claimants. Atcheson believes that the titles are the school's rightful claims.

And, so the UA 2009 Official Football Media Guide states that Alabama had 12 national championships prior to winning the 2010

BCS National Championship Game. The 2009, 2011, 2012, and 2015 titles extend the total number of national championships claimed by Alabama to 16. Eleven of Alabama's national championships were awarded by the wire-services (AP, Coaches' Poll) or by winning the BCS National Championship Game.

In January 2013, CNN suggested that Alabama was college football's new dynasty, and in May 2013, Athlon Sports ranked Alabama's ongoing dynasty as the fourth-best since 1934, behind Oklahoma (1948–58), Miami (1986–92), and Nebraska (1993–97). Watch out to the top three for sue as Alabama is not done yet.

Conference Championships

Alabama has a winning tradition. A gambler can get rich betting on Alabama games. The teams over the years have won a total of 30 conference championships; this includes 4 Southern Conference and 26 SEC Championships.

UA captured its 4 Southern Conference titles in 1924, 1925, 1926, and 1930. Alabama captured the first SEC title in 1933 and the team has won a total of 26 SEC Championships (1933, 1934, 1937, 1945, 1953, 1961, 1964, 1965, 1966, 1971, 1972, 1973, 1974, 1975, 1977, 1978, 1979, 1981, 1989, 1992, 1999, 2009, 2012, 2014, 2015, 2016).

The school has won more SEC football titles than any other school, including seven since the conference split into separate divisions and added the Championship Game in 1992. Alabama is the only SEC school to win an SEC Championship in every decade since the conference was founded in 1933. Alabama is synonymous with winning. Bear Bryant fit the Alabama winning tradition 100%. Nick Saban looks like a Bear Disciple.

Divisional Championships

Since the 1992 season, the SEC has been split into two divisions. Alabama competes in the SEC West. Alabama has won or shared 12 division titles, and has posted a 7-4 record in the SEC Championship Game as of 2016.

Those of us who root always or often for Alabama are seldom disappointed. What a football tradition. Roll Tide.

Heisman Trophy

One can certainly make the case that with such a phenomenal record, Alabama is either fully team-oriented and consistently lack individual talent; have been victimized by a biased voting system; or a simply victims of circumstance. No Alabama Heisman's during Bear Bryant's storied career? It just does not seem right.

There is always irony in every story. Bear Bryant did coach one Heisman winner, John David Crow. However, Crow played for the Texas Aggies when the Bear coached there. Bryant then moved on to Alabama and the Crimson Tide are quite pleased that he did.

I have to admit, I scoured for sources that could explain the lack of Heisman Trophies at Alabama. If you are reading this and you know, let me know, and in a future update to this book, I will more than likely include your perspective.

On December 12, 2009, the Heisman drought ended. Mark Ingram became Alabama's first Heisman Trophy winner. In the closest race ever, he edged out Stanford running back Toby Gerhart by 28 points. The previous best finish for an Alabama player occurred in 1993, when David Palmer finished 3rd in the Heisman voting. AJ McCarron finished as runner-up for the 2013 season. Derrick Henry became Alabama's second Heisman trophy winner on December 12, 2015.

Alabama fans are typically very happy

Overall, those of us who root always or often for Alabama are seldom disappointed. What a football tradition. Roll Tide.

Chapter 3 The Evolution of Modern American Football

Lots of playing before playing became official

The official agreed upon date for the first American-style college football game is November 6, 1869. If you can find a replay of this game someplace in the heavens, however, you would find it would not look much like football as we know it. But, it was not completely soccer or rugby either.

Before this game, teams were playing a rugby style similar to that played in Britain in the mid-19th century. At the time in the US, a derivative known as association football was also played. In both games, a football is kicked at a goal or run over a line. These styles were based on the varieties of English public school football games. Over time, as noted, the style of "football" play in America continued to evolve.

On November 6, 1869, the first football game in America featured Rutgers and Princeton. Before the teams were even on the field it was being plugged as the first college football game of all time. Notre Dame did have a rugby team at the time, but nobody at Notre Dame, from what I could find, was even thinking about the game of football.

The first game of intercollegiate football was a sporting battle between two neighboring schools on a plot of ground where the present-day Rutgers gymnasium now stands in New Brunswick, N.J. Rutgers won that first game, 6-4.

There were two teams of 25 men each and the rules were rugby-like, but different enough to make it very interesting and enjoyable.

Like today's football, there were many surprises; strategies needed to be employed; determination exhibited, and of course the players required physical prowess.

1st Game Rutgers 6 Princeton 4 College Field, New Brunswick, NJ

At 3 p.m. the 50 combatants as well as 100 spectators gathered on the field. Most sat on a low wooden fence and watched the athletes discard their hats, coats and vests. The players used their suspenders as belts. To give a unique look, Rutgers wore scarlet-colored scarfs, which they converted into turbans. This contrasted them with the bareheaded boys from Princeton.

Two members of each team remained more or less stationary near the opponent's goal in the hopes of being able to slip over and score from unguarded positions. Thus, the present day "sleeper" was conceived. The remaining 23 players were divided into groups of 11 and 12. While the 11 "fielders" lined up in their own territory as defenders, the 12 "bulldogs" carried the battle.

Each score counted as a "game" and 10 games completed the contest. Following each score, the teams changed direction. The ball could be advanced only by kicking or batting it with the feet, hands, heads or sides.

Rutgers put a challenge forward that three games were to be played that year. The first was played at New Brunswick and won by Rutgers. Princeton won the second game, but cries of "over-emphasis" prevented the third game in football's first year when faculties of both institutions protested on the grounds that the games were interfering with student studies.

This is an excerpt of the Rutgers account of the game on its web site. A person named Herbert gave this detailed account of the play in the first game:

"Though smaller on the average, the Rutgers players, as it developed, had ample speed and fine football sense. Receiving the ball, our men formed a perfect interference around it and with short, skillful kicks and dribbles drove it down the field. Taken by surprise, the Princeton men fought valiantly, but in five minutes we had gotten the ball through to our captains on the enemy's goal and S.G. Gano, '71 and G.R. Dixon, '73, neatly kicked it over. None thought of it, so far as I know, but we had without previous plan or thought evolved the play that became famous a few years later as 'the flying wedge'."

"Next period Rutgers bucked, or received the ball, hoping to repeat the flying wedge," Herbert's account continues. "But the first time we formed it Big Mike came charging full upon us. It was our turn for surprise. The Princeton battering ram made no attempt to reach the ball but, forerunner of the interference-breaking ends of today, threw himself into our mass play, bursting us apart, and bowing us over. Time and again Rutgers formed the wedge and charged; as often Big Mike broke it up. And finally, on one of these incredible break-ups a Princeton bulldog with a long accurate, perhaps lucky kick, sent the ball between the posts for the second score.

It was at this point that a Rutgers professor could stand it no longer. Waving his umbrella at the participants, he shrieked, "You will come to no Christian end!"

Herbert's account of the game continues: "The fifth and sixth goals went to Rutgers. The stars of the latter period of play, in the memory of the players after the lapse of many years, were "Big

Mike" and Large (former State Senator George H. Large of Flemington, another Princeton player) ...

The University of the State of Alabama did not get into the football act until the early 1890's. At this time, the rules of rugby kept changing to accommodate the infatuation for the Americanized style of "football" play that would ultimately become the American game of football.

Walter Camp: the father of American football?

Walter Camp was a very well-known rugby player from Yale. In today's world, he would have been characterized as a rugby hero. It was his love of the game, his knowledge of the game as it was played, and his innovative mind that caused him to take the evolution of football even further. He pioneered the changes to the rules of rugby that slowly transformed the sport into the new game of American Football.

The rule changes that were introduced to the rugby and association style of play were mostly those authored by Camp, who was also a Hopkins School graduate. For his original efforts, Walter Camp today is considered to be the "Father of American Football". Among the important changes brought to the game were the introduction of a line of scrimmage; down-and-distance rules; and the legalization of interference (blocking).

There was no such thing in those days as a forward pass and so the legalization of interference in 1880 football permitted blocking for runners. The forward pass would add another dimension to the game that made it much different than rugby or association football.

Soon after the early football changes, in the late nineteenth and into the early twentieth centuries, more game-play type developments were introduced by college coaches. The list is like a who's who of early American College Football. Coaches, such as Eddie Cochems, Amos Alonzo Stagg, Parke H. Davis, Knute Rockne, John Heisman, and Glenn "Pop" Warner helped introduce and then take advantage of the newly introduced forward pass. College football as well as professional football, were introduced prior to the 20th century. Fans were lured into watching again and again once they saw the game played.

College football especially grew in popularity despite the existence of pro-football. It became the dominant version of the sport of football in the United States. It was this way for the entire first half of the 20th century. Bowl games made the idea of football even more exciting in the college ranks. Rivalries grew and continued and the fans loved it! This great football tradition brought a national audience to college football games that still dominates the sports world today.

This book has little to do with pro-football or any other sport. However, there is no denying that the greatest college football players more often than not eventually found their fortunes in professional football. Pro football can be traced back to the season that Notre Dame brought forth a real football team after a two-year lapse from its last half-Rugby season in 1889.

It was 1892 when William "Pudge" Heffelfinger signed a $500 contract to play for the Allegheny Athletic Association against the Pittsburgh Athletic Club.

Twenty-eight years later, the American Professional Football Association was formed. This league changed its name to the National Football League (NFL) just two years later. Eventually, the NFL became the major league of American football. Originally, just a sport played in Midwestern industrial towns in the United States, professional football eventually became a national phenomenon.

We all know this because from August to February, in America, many of us are glued to our TV sets or chained to our seats in some of the most intriguing pro-football stadiums in America.

Rules and Penalties

The big problem players from different teams and different geographies had when playing early American-style football in college was that the style of play was not standardized. The rulebooks were not yet written or were at best incomplete and disputable.

A rule over here, for example, would be a penalty over there. And, so in the 1870's there was a lot of work to try to make all games to be played by the same rules. There were minor rule changes such as team size was reduced from 25 to 20 but of course over the years, this and all other rules continued to evolve. For years, there was no such thing as a running touchdown. The only means of scoring was to bat or kick the ball through the opposing team's goal.

Early rugby rules were the default. The field size was rugby style at 140 yards by 70 yards v 120 X 53 1/3 (including end zones) in today's football game. There was plenty of room to huff and puff and almost get lost. There were no breaks per se for long periods. Instead of fifteen minute quarters, the game was more like Rugby and Soccer with 45 minute halves played continuously.

In 1873 to put some order to the game, Columbia, Princeton. Rutgers, and Yale got together in a hotel in New York City and wrote down the first set of intercollegiate football rules. They changed a few things along the way but the end product was a much more standard way of playing football games. Rather than use the home team's rules, all teams then were able to play by the same rules

Harvard did not to comply with rules

For its own reasons, Harvard chose not to attend the rules conference. Instead, it played all of its games using the Harvard code of rules. Harvard therefore had a difficult time scheduling games. In 1874, to get a game, Harvard agreed to play McGill University from Montreal Canada. They had rules that even Harvard had never seen. For example, any player could pick up the ball and run with it, anytime he wished.

Another McGill rule was that they would count tries (the act of grounding the football past the opponent's goal line. Since there was no end zone, which technically makes a football field of today 120 yards long, a touchdown gave no points. Instead, it provided the chance to kick a free goal from the field. If the kick were missed, the touchdown did not count.

In 1874 McGill and Harvard played a two-game series. Each team could play 11 men per side. This was in deep contrast to the even earlier days of college football before standard rules when games were played with 25, 20, 15, or 11 men on a side.

The first game was played with a round ball using what were known as the "Boston" rules (Harvard). The next day, the teams played using the McGill rules, which included McGill's oval ball which was much like an American football, and it featured the ability to pick up the ball and run with it.

Harvard enjoyed this experience especially the idea of "the try" which had not been used in American football. Eventually, the try evolved into the American idea of a touchdown and points were given when a try was successful.

Not all the rules lasted the duration and some were very strange by today's standards. One of the most perplexing rules was that a man could run with the ball only while an opponent chose to pursue him. When a tackler abandoned the ball-carrier, the latter had to stop, and was forced to kick, pass or even throw away what was called "his burden."

McGill has a great account of this match on their web site. Type *mcgill web site football against Harvard* into your search engine.

Their players wore no protective pads. Woolen jerseys covered the torso, while white trousers encased the players' legs. Some trousers were short and some were long. It did not seem to matter for the game. A number of the men wore what they called black "football turbans" which were the ancestors of the modern helmet; others chose to wear white canvas hats.

The Harvard players wore undershirts made of gauze. Think about that for a while. They also wore what were called *full length gymnasium costumes*. They also wore light baseball shoes. Most of the team wore handkerchiefs, which were knotted about their heads.

The gauze undershirts were a trick. There was strategy in this choice of top uniform. When a player was first tackled, the gauze would be demolished and the next opponent would have nothing to grab other than "slippery human flesh." Harvard won this game by a score of 3-0

The next go at playing by the rules was when Harvard took on Tufts University on June 4, 1875. This was the first American college football game played using rules similar to the McGill/Harvard contest. Tufts won this game. Despite the loss, Harvard continued pushing McGill style football and challenged Yale.

The Bulldog team accepted under a compromise rule set that included some Yale soccer rules and Harvard rugby rules. They used 15 players per team. It was November 13, 1875 for this first meeting of Harvard v Yale. Harvard won 4-0. Walter Camp attended the game and the following year he played in the game as a Yale Bulldog.

Camp was determined to avenge Yale's defeat. Onlookers from Princeton, who saw this Harvard / Yale game loved it so much, they brought it back to Princeton where it was quickly adopted as the preferred version of football.

Once Walter Camp caught onto the rugby-style rules, history says he became a fixture at the Massasoit House conventions. Here the rules of the game were debated and changed appropriately. From these meetings, Camp's rule changes as well as others were adopted.

Having eleven players instead of fifteen aided in opening the game and it emphasized speed over strength. When Camp attended in 1878, this motion was rejected but it passed in the 1880 meeting. The line of scrimmage and the snap from center to the quarterback also passed in 1880.

Originally the snap occurred by a kick from the center, but this was later modified so the ball would be snapped with the hands either as a pass back (long snap) or a direct snap from the center.

It was Camp's new scrimmage rules, however, which according to many, revolutionized the game, though it was not always to increase speed. In fact, Princeton was known to use line of scrimmage plays to slow the game, making incremental progress towards the end zone much like today during each down.

Camp's original idea was to increase scoring, but in fact the rule was often misused to maintain control of the ball for the entire game. The negative effect was that there were many slow and unexciting contests. This too would be fixed with the idea of the first down coming into play.

In 1982, at the rules meeting, Camp proposed that a team be given three downs to advance the ball five yards. These rules were called the down and distance rules. Along with the notion of the line of scrimmage, these rules transformed the game of rugby into the distinct sport of American football.

Among other significant rule changes, in 1881, the field size was reduced to its modern dimensions of 120 by 53 1/3 yards (109.7 by 48.8 meters). Camp was central to these significant rule changes that ultimately defined American football. Camp's next quest was to address scoring anomalies. His first cut was to give four points for a touchdown and two points for kicks after touchdowns; two points for safeties, and five points for field goals. The notion of the foot in football /rugby explains Camp's rationale.

In 1887, game time was fixed at two halves of 45 minutes each. Additionally college games would have two paid officials known as a referee and an umpire, for each game. In 1888, the rules permitted tackling below the waist and then in 1889, the officials were given whistles and stopwatches to better control the game.

An innovation that many list as most significant to making American football uniquely American was the legalization of blocking opponents, which back then was called "interference." This tactic had been highly illegal under the rugby-style rules and in rugby today, it continues to be illegal.

The more those who know soccer and football find rugby to be more like soccer.

Though *offsides* is a penalty infraction today, *offsides* in the 1880's in rugby was very much the same as *offsides* in soccer. The prohibition of blocking in a rugby game is in fact because of the game's strict enforcement of its *offsides* rule.

Similar to soccer, this rule prohibits any player on the team with possession of the ball to loiter between the ball and the goal. Blocking continues as a basic element of modern American football, with many complex schemes having been developed and implemented over the years, including zone blocking and pass blocking.

Camp stayed active in rule making for most of his life. He had the honor of personally selecting an annual All-American team every year from 1889 through 1924. Camp passed away in 1925. The Walter Camp Football Foundation continues to select All-American teams in his honor.

With many rule changes as noted, as American style rugby became more defined as American football, more and more colleges adopted football as part of their sports programs. Most of the schools were from the Eastern US. It was not until 1879 that the University of Michigan became the first school west of Pennsylvania to establish a bona-fide American-style college football team.

Back then, football teams played whenever they could in the fall or the spring. For example, Michigan's first game was in late spring, near the end of what we would call the academic year. On May 30, 1879 Michigan beat Racine College 1–0 in a game played in Chicago. In 1887, Michigan and Notre Dame played their first football game, which did not benefit from Camp's rules.

The first night time game

It was not until September 28, 1892 that the first nighttime football game was played. Mansfield State Normal played Wyoming Seminary in Mansfield, Pennsylvania. These schools are close to where I live. The game ended at a "declared" half-time in a 0–0 tie. It had become too dark to play.

Wyoming Seminary was not a college and to this day it is not a college. I live about five miles from the school. It is a private college preparatory school located in the Wyoming Valley of Northeastern Pennsylvania. During the time period in which the game was played, it was common for a college and high school to play each other in football—a practice that of course has long since been discontinued.

The reason that it got too dark to play, ironically was not because the game began at dusk. Mansfield had brought in a lighting system that was far too inadequate for game play. This historical game lasted only 20 minutes and there were only 10 plays. Both sides agreed to end at half-time with the score at 0-0. Though it may seem humorous today, for safety reasons, the game was declared ended in a 0-0 tie after several players had an unfortunate run-in with a light pole.

Mansfield and Wyoming Seminary are thus enshrined in football history as having played in the first night game ever in "college football." History and football buffs get together once a year to celebrate the game in what they call "Fabulous 1890's Weekend." This historic game is reenacted exactly as it occurred play by play just as the actual game is recorded in history. Fans who watch the game are sometimes known to correct players (actually actors) when they deviate from the original scripted plays. Now, that shows both a love of the game and a love of history.

Mansfield and Wyoming Seminary's game added additional fame to both schools when the 100th anniversary of the game just happened to occur on Monday, September 28, 1992. Monday Night Football celebrated "100 years of night football" with its regularly scheduled game between the Los Angeles Raiders and the Kansas City Chiefs at Arrowhead Stadium. The Chiefs won 27–7 in front of 77,486 fans. How about that?

More football history was recorded when Army played Navy in 1893. This was during the second season of Alabama football. In this game, we have the first documented use of a football helmet by a player in a game. Joseph M. Reeves had been kicked in the head in a prior football game. He was warned by his doctor that he risked death if he continued to play football.

We all know how tough the Midshipmen and Black Nights (Cadets) are regardless of who they may be playing. Rather than end his football playing days prematurely. Reeves discussed his need with a shoemaker in Annapolis who crafted a leather helmet for the player to wear for the rest of the season.

Football conferences

Things were happening very quickly in the new sport of football. Organization and rules became the mantra for this fledgling sport. It was being defined while it was being played. Formal college football conferences were just around the corner. In fact, the Southeastern Conference and the Atlantic Coast Conference both got started in1894.

The Southeastern Conference (SEC) was established on December 8 and 9, 1932, when the thirteen members of the Southern Conference located west and south of the Appalachian Mountains left to form their own conference.

Ten of the thirteen founding members have remained in the conference since its inception: the University of Alabama, Auburn University, the University of Florida, the University of Georgia, the University of Kentucky, Louisiana State University ("LSU"), the

University of Mississippi ("Ole Miss"), Mississippi State University, the University of Tennessee, and Vanderbilt University.

Many, throughout the country see the SEC as a money-printing, championship-winning behemoth across college sports. It is home to 14 schools that compete in just about every sport across college athletics, it has its own television network and it inspires regional pride unrivaled across the nation.

The forward pass

None of Walter Camp's rules for American Football included the most innovative notion of them all – the forward pass. Many believe that the first forward pass in football occurred on October 26, 1895 in a game between Georgia and North Carolina. Out of desperation, the ball was thrown by the North Carolina back Joel Whitaker instead of having been punted. George Stephens, a teammate caught the ball.

Despite what most may think or surmise, it was Camp again when he was a player at Yale, who executed the first game-time forward pass for a touchdown. During the Yale-Princeton game, while Camp was being tackled, he threw a football forward to Yale's Oliver Thompson, who sprinted to a touchdown. The Princeton Tigers naturally protested and there appeared to be no precedent for a referee decision.

Like many things in football including a game-beginning coin-toss, the referee in this instance tossed a coin, and then he made his decision to allow the touchdown.

Hidden ball trick

Dome one-time tricks have not survived football. For example, on November 9, 1895 Auburn Coach John Heisman executed a hidden ball trick. Quarterback Reynolds Tichenor was able to gain Auburn's only touchdown in a 6 to 9 loss to Vanderbilt. This also was the first game in the south that was decided by a field goal.

The trick was simple but would be illegal today. When the ball was snapped, it went to a halfback. The play was closely masked and well screened. The halfback then thrust the ball under the back of the quarterback's (Tichenor) jersey. Then the halfback would crash into the line. After the play, Tichenor "simply trotted away to a touchdown."

The end of college football?

Football was never a game for the light of heart. You had to be tough physically and tough mentally to compete. Way back in 1906, for example complaints were many about the violence in American Football. It got so bad that universities on the West Coast, led by California and Stanford, replaced the sport with rugby union.

At the time, the future of American college football, a very popular sport enjoyed by fans nationwide was in doubt. The schools that eliminated football and replaced it with rugby union believed football would be gone and rugby union would eventually be adopted nationwide.

Soon other schools followed this travesty and made the switch. Eventually, due to the perception that West Coast football was an inferior game played by inferior men when compared to the rough and tumble East Coast, manhood prevailed in the West over the inclination to make the game mild.

The many tough East Coast and Midwest teams had shrugged off the loss of the few teams out West and they had continued to play American style football.

And, so the available pool of rugby union "football" teams to play remained small. The Western colleges therefore had to schedule games against local club teams and they reached out to rugby union powers in Australia, New Zealand, and especially, due to its proximity, Canada.

The famous Stanford and California game continued as rugby. To make it seem important. The winner was invited by the British Columbia Rugby Union to a tournament in Vancouver over the Christmas holidays. The winner of that tournament was rewarded with the Cooper Keith Trophy. Nobody in America cared. Eventually the West Coast came back to football.

Nonetheless the situation of injury and death in football persisted and though there was a lot of pushback, it came to a head in 1905 when there were 19 fatalities nationwide. President Theodore Roosevelt, a tough guy himself, is reported as having threatened to shut down the game nationwide if drastic changes were not made. Sports historians however, dispute that Roosevelt ever intervened.

What is certified, however, is that on October 9, 1905, the President held a meeting of football representatives from Harvard, Yale, and Princeton. The topic was eliminating and reducing injuries and the President according to the record, never threatened to ban football.

The fact is that Roosevelt lacked the authority to abolish football but more importantly, he was a big fan and wanted the game to continue. The little Roosevelts also loved the sport and were playing football at the college and secondary levels at the time.

Meanwhile, there were more rule changes such as the notion of reducing the number of scrimmage plays to earn a first down from four to three in an attempt to reduce injuries. The LA Times reported an increase in punts in an experimental game and thus considered the game much safer than regular play. Football lovers did not accept the new rule because it was not "conducive to the sport."

Because nobody wanted players injured or killed in a game, on December 28, 1905, 62 schools met in New York City to discuss major rule changes to make the game safer. From this meeting, the Intercollegiate Athletic Association of the United States, later named the National Collegiate Athletic Association (NCAA), was formed.

The forward pass is legalized

One rule change that was introduced in 1906 was devised to open up the game and thus reduce injury. This new rule introduced the legal forward pass. Though it was underutilized for years, this proved to be one of the most important rule changes in the establishment of the modern game.

Because of these 1905-1906 reforms, mass formation plays in which many players joined together became illegal when forward passes became legal. Bradbury Robinson, playing for visionary coach Eddie Cochems at St. Louis University, is recorded as throwing the first legal pass in a September 5, 1906, game against Carroll College at Waukesha.

Later changes were in the minutia category but they added discipline and safety to the game without destroying its rugged character. For example, in 1910, came the new requirement that at least seven offensive players be on the line of scrimmage at the time of the snap, that there be no pushing or pulling, and that interlocking interference (arms linked or hands on belts and uniforms) was not allowed. These changes accomplished their intended purpose of greatly reducing the potential for collision injuries.

As noted previously, great coaches emerged in the ranks who took advantage of these sweeping changes. Amos Alonzo Stagg, for example, introduced such innovations as the huddle, the tackling dummy, and the pre-snap shift. Other coaches, such as Pop Warner and Notre Dame's Knute Rockne, introduced new strategies that still remain part of the game.

Many other rules changes and coaching innovations came about before 1940. They all had a profound impact on the game, mostly in opening up the passing game, but also in making the game safer to play without diminishing its quality.

For example, in 1914, the first roughing-the-passer penalty was implemented. In 1918, the rules on eligible receivers were loosened to allow eligible players to catch the ball anywhere on the field. The previously more restrictive rules allowed passes only in certain areas of the field.

Scoring rules also changed which brought the scoring into the modern era. For example, field goals were lowered from five to three points in 1909 and touchdowns were raised from four to six points in 1912.

Star Players

Star players emerged in both the collegiate and professional ranks including Jim Thorpe, Red Grange, and Bronko Nagurski. There were also other stars. These three in particular were able to move from college to the fledgling NFL and they helped turn it into a successful league. Notable sportswriter Grantland Rice helped popularize the sport of football with his poetic descriptions of games and colorful nicknames for the game's biggest players, including Notre Dame's "Four Horsemen" backfield and Fordham University's linemen, known as the "Seven Blocks of Granite".

Jim Thorpe, Circa 1915

The Heisman

Jay Berwanger (above) was the 1st Heisman Winner. In 1935, New York City's Downtown Athletic Club awarded its first Heisman Trophy to University of Chicago halfback Jay Berwanger (left).

He was also the first ever NFL Draft pick in 1936. The trophy continues to this day to recognize the nation's "most outstanding" college football player. It has become one of the most coveted awards in all of American sports.

As professional football became a national television phenomenon, college football did as well. In the 1950s, Notre Dame, which had a large national following, formed its own network to broadcast its games, but by and large the sport still retained a mostly regional following.

New formations and play sets continued to be developed by innovative coaches and their staffs. Emory Bellard from the University of Texas, developed a three-back option style offense known as the wishbone. Bear Bryant of Alabama became a preacher of the wishbone.

The strategic opposite of the wishbone is called the spread offense. Some teams have managed to adapt with the times to keep winning consistently. In the rankings of the most victorious programs, Michigan, Texas, and Notre Dame are ranked first, second, and third in total wins.

And so, that is as far as we will take it in this chapter about the early evolution of football. With so many conferences and sports associations as well as pro, college, high school, and mini sports, something tells me we have not yet seen our last rule change.

Chapter 4 Perspective on the Great Players in Alabama Football

Introduction

There are many leaders of the world who think the gold standard is unusable for currency. Over time, these leaders have had their way in most countries including the US. Today US currency value floats with the value of what it can purchase. There is no gold standard for US currency. The US now has a fiat money system, meaning the dollar's value is not linked to any specific asset. It is thus tricky trying to figure out what a dollar is worth. So, how can we find the relative value of a football player, which is very subjective when we cannot find a standard to measure the value of currency, a very objective notion.

Consequently, we can readily conclude that It tricky trying to name the best players in the history of the University of Alabama football program history as there is no one standard to use – rushing yards, sacks, interceptions, pass completions. And, of course there are the intangibles such as desire, natural ability, etc. I think you see my point.

We learned in this book that the Alabama football program dates from 1892. It boasts of having 120 or more players who were named first-team All-American over 150 times, and 240 or more players who landed all-conference honors over 320 times. The list of Alabama greats is large indeed. Moreover, few of us alive today saw the first game in 1892 and the last game on January 9, 2017 or later. Nobody can know it all for sure?

Alabama has won so many trophies that a couple of years ago the Bryant Museum ran a humorous ad campaign. The idea was that the Crimson Tide could consider using some of the "revered artifacts" for novel gifts such as paper weights, back scratchers, door jams, etc. The bottom line is how can a mere human define best as it pertains to any player from any position?

Do you base it on statistics? Would a player have had to been named an All-American or to a Hall of Fame to be considered? Can a ratio be created so that so many sacks equal so many receptions? How would we compare players from different eras?

Would being the biggest icon count? If so, quarterback Joe Namath would of course have to be included, and probably Kenny Stabler as well, even though neither is in the College Football Hall of Fame. Yet, they are two of my most favorite Alabama players. I bet there are others with differing opinions.

Why not use most awards? There would have to be a place for offensive lineman Barrett Jones. Should continual success be the criterion? Quarterback AJ McCarron and linebacker Woodrow Lowe would be right there at the top.

I am convinced that Consequently, if 100 different people put a list of Alabama's best 100 players together, there would be 100 different results with different rankings. Surely, you can go to the Internet and find many lists that compare Alabama players and deliver results like as if they are definitely correct. I encourage you to make your own list and compare.

For this chapter, the standard is simple. I like the method but you might not. In some ways, it is like being on a playground picking teams. These are the players that I'd want on my team —the players who have to be considered among the best to ever play for the Crimson Tide. Of course, on your list, which would be different than mine, the players would be different and they would more than likely be picked in a different sequence.

I expect this to be a living book and I suspect I will receive a lot of input about this topic and I can see more names being added as the years go by. And, they may not all be mew players.

I have picked my players over the full research process of writing this book. I have them all written down already. My list is categorized and as complete as it will be until the next edition of the book.

I first created a tentative list of great talent. I then scoured my list of "***Grea*t** Alabama Football Players." I did not presume to know the **greatest** of them or the ranking of any of the players, I then picked an extended team and I think you would agree we could beat a most if not all of the other teams out there from all over the football ages.

I then categorized the list by position. In this way, I can present something fun to read to you. This list is now textually formatted with pictures and it is categorize by general position. The sequence of the players within the categories is random with very little of "I like that guy" help when a name is placed in the category.

If it were based on who would be on my mind first, it might have been Kenny "The Snake" Stabler on top of the list and Joe Namath second, and Bart Starr, third, or maybe the same names in a different sequence. But, the list is random by position. I hope you find the list enjoyable and that you enjoy reading about some of the great players in Alabama football. Sure most of them would be in anybody else's greatest list but I did not do it that way. At a minimum it gives the readers of this book something to chew the fat about when you get together, have a few beers, and compare notes:

Chapter 5 Great Alabama Quarterbacks

Harry Gilmer

Harry Gilmer is on everybody's "greatest" list so I would not ever consider leaving him off my "great" list. During World War II, Harry headed up what was called "The War Babies," a group of players who, for the most part, could not serve in the military for one reason or another. Harry went on to have a prestigious career. The renowned sportswriter Grantland Rice called him, "the greatest college passer I've ever seen."

In his sophomore year, Harry Gilmer led the nation in passing touchdowns (13) and was second in total offense (1,457 yards). In his junior year, Gilmer led the nation in punt returns with a 14.5

average on 37 returns. He was a versatile quarterback wo in his spare time played defensive back. .

He was resilient and had the good fortune of being drafted by the Washington Redskins. Before that, Gilmer was the 9146 Rose Bowl MVP, and he was the first overall draft pick in 1948. What a guy!

Harry Gilmer ended his career as Alabama's all-time leader in rushing (1,673 yards), passing (2,894 yards), punt returns (13.5 average), kickoff returns (28.7 yard average.) and interceptions. He also passed for 26 touchdowns and ran for 24 more. If time stood still, Harry would won all those records today. Nobody can deny, however, for his day, Harry was great and at quarterback he was definitely the greatest.

Besides his explosive offensive talents, Gilmer also punted for the Tide with an average of 36.4 yards per punt. He could do anything or so it seemed. He also played defensive back. Harry Gilmer is not a name that every Crimson Tide fan knows, but it's a name every Crimson Tide fan should know.

Harry was born in Birmingham Alabama in 1926 and went to Woodlawn High School. He was a great innovator and was best known for his jumping in the air and then passing the ball. Check out the picture.

Gilmer played football as a child with kids that were much older than him so he learned quickly. To combat the height difference, he would jump in the air as he threw the ball. Harry Gilmer originated the jump pass. It was not Tim Tebow.

Gilmer had an enormous career with the Tide. Some think his biggest success with the Crimson Tide might have been leading the Tide to the 1946 Rose Bowl where he helped to beat USC 34-14. Gilmer was the MVP of the Rose Bowl that year.

Gilmer was the SEC player of the year, all SEC, and an All-American in 1945. In addition to being picked first for the NFL draft, he was invited to the pro bowl twice. He then coached the Detroit Lions for a year after he retired as a player in the NFL.

Chapter 5 Great Alabama Quarterbacks. 49

Harry Gilmer... do you got that... one of the best ever at any position.

Bart Starr

Ole # 15, Bart Starr was born on January 9, 1934 in Montgomery Alabama and he "ain't never been nothin' but a winner". My dad and I loved watching Bart Starr and the Packers win one after another on Sundays on our 1956 Admiral B/W tube style TV.

Some of today's NFL players might claim that all they do is win, but for Bart Starr that was the reality… but it took him a little time to get there. Starr's star time at Alabama was an up and down affair plagued by injuries that kept him sidelined for most of his junior year, which is why he isn't higher on the other folks' lists of the greats.

Once he got to the NFL though, everything changed. Starr was so poorly used at Alabama by Jennings Whitworth, who occupies the bottom of most folk's Alabama head coaching list, that his record was not good enough for a pro-tryout. If it were not for a friend Bart Starr would have been a successful businessman someplace.

He got his shot at the NFL only because he was recommended to the Green Bay Packers personnel director by Alabama's basketball coach Johnny Dee. Great coaches in all sports can recognize talent. Johnny Dee, the great Alabama basketball coach knew Bart Starr had that certain something. Dee coached basketball at Alabama and also at Notre Dame. He knew how to win.

Coach Drew was replaced by Coach Whitworth who changed everything about the Alabama football program but especially its winning tradition. Bart Starr whose injury was severe had played for Drew as an underclassman and did quite well. When it came his time, however, as a senior after being injured, the new coach decided he wanted the team to run the ball and not be so flashy with the passes. Bart Starr was a great passer. Only when it was a last resort did Starr play in his senior year so there was little for the pros to find in his record to make him a good selection.

Thanks to Johnny Dee, Bart Starr had a 9-1 playoff record in the NFL and led the Packers to five championships and Super Bowls I and II. Starr was the MVP of both Super Bowls in which he played. He went to four Pro Bowls and was also the NFL's MVP in 1966. All of this after what some might say was an injury-plagued mediocre college career at Alabama and being drafted 200th overall in the 17th round of the 1956 draft.

Alabama claims Bart Starr, one of the greatest football players of all time as one of its own. Starr is the perfect example of a player who didn't reach his full potential until he got to the NFL. Starr may not be remembered for wild success on the field at Alabama, but he is undoubtably one of the great quarterbacks who played at Alabama. There are none who can always claim that they were always a Starr.

Starr also coached the Green Bay Packers from 1975-1983. How's that for a record.

Pat Trammell

As soon as I realized that Pat Trammell from Scottsboro, AL was Bear Bryant's first quarterback and Bear Bryant's first star, I asked myself how he could be denied his spot on this list of Alabama "greats." He cannot be denied and so he won't be denied.

Before committing to Alabama, Trammell had planned to play for Coach Bobby Dodd at Georgia Tech. But his plans changed when Coach Bear Bryant mentioned to Trammell's family on a visit to his home that if Pat came to Alabama, he'd come too.

During the 1959 season, sophomore Pat Trammell led the Tide in total offense and in 1960 he led the team in scoring. He is an unsung hero was often an Alabama hero. He is a hero no matter how you might try to cut it.

In 1961 Pat Trammell led the Alabama Crimson Tide to a perfect season as its field general and he led them to a unanimous national championship. It was the program's first championship since the leadership of coach Frank Thomas.

Trammell was the player chosen to accompany Coach Bryant to New York for the presentation of the MacArthur Trophy. Bryant and Trammel accepted the trophy from President John F. Kennedy on national television at a black tie gala hosted by Bob Hope.

Trammell was the 1961 SEC Player of the Year and an NCAA Academic All-American. His hand and foot prints are cemented in front of Denny Chimes as a permanent captain for the 1961 team. He is one of Alabama's greats. He was Bear's first QB.

Trammel was so good that Green Bay Packers coach Vince Lombardi tried to get Alabama coach Bear Bryant to convince Pat to play for the Packers after graduation. Bear Bryant gave Trammel all the credit in the world as a human being as Coach Bryant told Coach Lombardi that Trammell was too smart. Pat Trammel completed an undergraduate degree summa cum laude in physical chemistry and went on to medical school and in his life saved many lives.

They tell me that two Alabama records still belong to Pat Trammell – lowest interception percentage for a single season (1.5%, 1960) and lowest career interception percentage. If the recordsmeisters find that I got this wrong, please let me know and I will fix this but I know you know that we do the best we can in life as there is no better that we can do without help from guys like you and me. When the Bear thinks somebody is a "great," who could vote against such a nominee.

AJ McCarron

AJ McCarron signed up for a tour of duty at Alabama U in 2009 after a standout career at St. Paul's Episcopal in Mobile, AL. He redshirted in the 2009 season, then he backed up Greg McElroy during the 2010 campaign. McCarron was a team player and came ready when the coach called him.

In 2011 McCarron played well against Kent State and Penn State to secure the starting job over Phillip Sims and spent the next three seasons as the first face of the Alabama offense.

The 2011 Tide offense was run-first on the back of Trent Richardson, giving McCarron time to settle into his role as a starter and ease his way to success. His performance in the National Championship game against LSU (23-34, 234 yds, 0 TD, 0 INT) earned him Offensive MVP honors in a W (21-0) effort..

A 291 pass streak that started in 2011 and ended in the 2012 season is an SEC record for most consecutive pass attempts without an interception.

Amari Cooper's arrival in 2012 gave McCarron his highest yards per attempt for a season in his career. AJ led the country in passer efficiency and set a school record for single-season passing touchdowns.

McCarron threw a 44-yard touchdown to Cooper to take the lead against UGA to clinch a berth in a second national championship game. He was again nearly flawless against Notre Dame in the championship game, throwing for four touchdowns. His only negative in terms of being on the "Great" list is that his legacy has not matured. His reality has overwhelmed his legacy before his time. Amen to AJ McCarron.

In 2013, McCarron was an all-SEC selection. He had broken Greg McElroy's school record for single-season passing yards, and he became Alabama's all-time passing yards leader. He won the Maxwell Award and the Johnny Unitas Golden Arm Award and finished second in voting for the Heisman Trophy. Perhaps he should have been # 1.

McCarron was selected by the Cincinnati Bengals in the fifth round of the 2014 NFL Draft. He took over the starting role at the end of the regular season in his first year to replace an injured Andy Dalton. If you can play for Alabama, you can play anywhere!

Kenny Stabler

My father-in-law wore a Kenny Stabler T-shirt in proper rotation and an Oakland Raiders hat for years as "the snake" at the Raiders was his favorite player on his favorite team. They guys at the "Legion" loved his attire. Stanley Piotroski died too quickly after open heart surgery one weekend that I was at a national college football game. I thought Dad had it made already and would be joining us at the games soon. I was wrong. The best laid plans of mice and men gang oft aglay. He loved Stabler. Dad "played" at Iwo Jimo and spent too much time bagging American bodies to actually have a sense of humor. Yet he had a great sense of humor.

He told me what a non-conformist Mr. Stabler was and he loved the Snake to pieces. So, I have an affinity for the Snake, and I hope this Alabama great is now having one-on-ones with Smokey Piotroski among some of his buddies in the land of football immortals.

Wouldn't you like to be the guy on the cover of Sports Illustrated when their hottest editions had nothing to do with bathing suits? Kenny "The Snake" Stabler was Alabama Crimson Tide royalty. The Snake was the kind of football player that Alabama fans love. He was tough, talented, and cocky.

Kenny Stabler was born in Foley, Alabama on December 25, 1945…so when you open your family presents on Christmas morning, you can always think of the Snake.

Stabler was one of a kind. He was an extremely talented all-around athlete in high school. He loved football the best. Mr. Stabler turned down contract offers from the Houston Astros and the New York Yankees to go to Alabama so he could play top-notch football.

He came to Alabama in 1964, but Kenny Stabler couldn't play on the varsity because at the time the NCAA forbid freshmen from playing. Some see this as proof that in many ways the NCAA has never made much sense. Stabler didn't play much in 1965 either as he was backing up Steve Sloan. If you know your football, you must be saying, "Holy Cow Batman, Bear Bryant had Joe Namath, Steve Sloan, and Kenny Stabler on his roster all at the same time." Now that sure is something.

In his first season as the Crimson Tide's quarterback Ken Stabler helped the Tide finish with an 11-0 record and he contributed mightily to a blowout of Nebraska in the Sugar Bowl.

Kenny Stabler's Senior season didn't go as well for him. He wound up getting kicked off the team for a while for cutting class. That year, however, did contain what would become known as "The Run in the Mud." While trailing Auburn in an Iron Bowl Stabler pleased Alabama fans forever when he ran for 53 yards to win the game. Bear Bryant said he could watch that play forever.

Stabler was well known as a great NFL Quarterback for the Oakland Raiders from 1970-1979. The scrambling lefty was fun to watch. He helped the Raiders win Super Bowl XI. Stabler was called into action in four NFL Pro Bowls as well. He was finally inducted into the Football Hall of Fame.

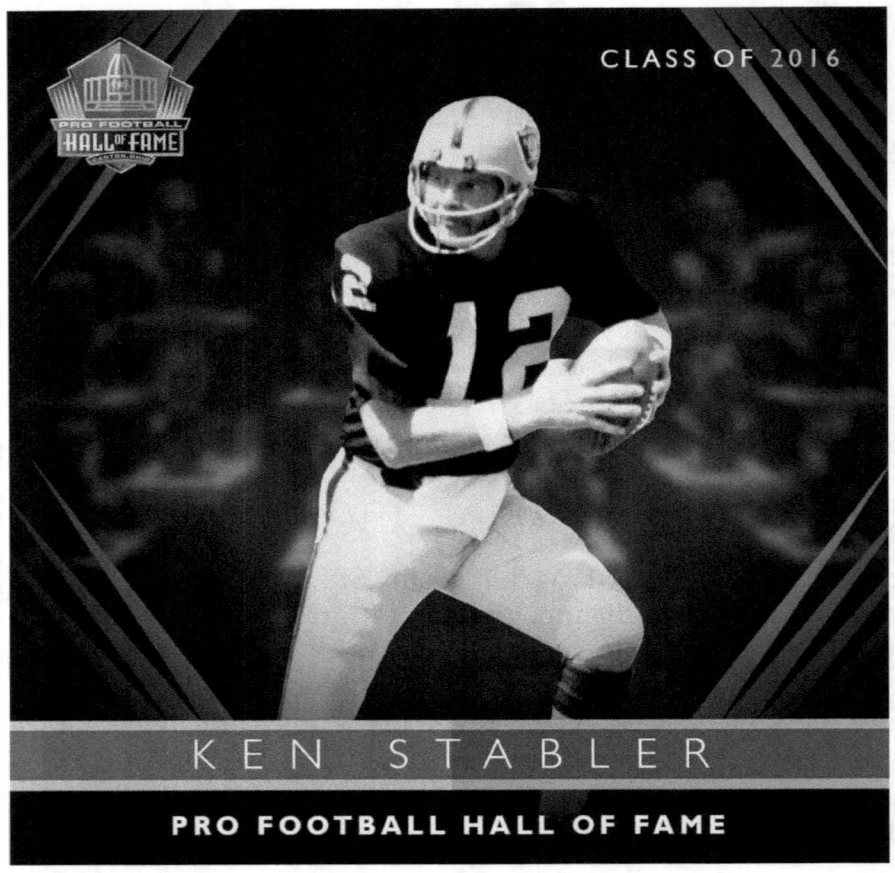

When he finished playing, Kenny Stabler joined Eli Gold as the color commentator for Alabama football on the radio until 2008. Listening to the Snake became a favorite pastime of many Alabama fans during the 2000s.

Besides being a full-time rascal, Kenny Stabler had a soft side and took the time to write a children's book called "Roll Tide!"

Sadly the Snake passed away on July 8, 2015. He was just 69 years old. He will be missed by many including yours truly. Save a place for Kenny under your Christmas tree each year and at the family table. Ask him how his new buddy Smokey Piotroski is doing?

Joe Namath

No description necessary

Joe Namath of Beaver Falls, PA played for the Crimson Tide from 1961-1964. By the way, his home town population was just 8,987 at the time of the 2010 census. Beaver Falls swells way past its natural size when Joe Namath comes back to his home town. They sure love Joe Namath in Beaver Falls. That says a lot about the man.

In 1969, the town had a celebration for Mr. Namath as he was celebrating his own great fortune in pro-football after a fine college career with the Crimson Tide. The Mayor presented Joe with the keys to the City. Namath is an overall good guy and has a lot of affection for a lot of people including his family and his football coach. On Joe Namath Day in Beaver Falls, the regulars rode with him in the provided limousine. He has a great sense of humor and he can recall at the time of the presentation of the keys having some other thoughts:

There Are No Coal Mines In Beaver Falls

By Joe Namath with Dick Schaap

"At the big dinner the mayor of Beaver Falls, Howard Marshall, presented me with the keys to the city. It was nice of him to do that, but by then I would have preferred a glass of Scotch."

I was going home, back to Beaver Falls, on May 23, 1969, to celebrate the first, and possibly last, "Joe Namath Day." I don't think it'll ever be a national holiday. I had just a small group with me—a lawyer, a public-relations man, a television crew, half a dozen photographers and writers, a couple of teammates, a few friends, and two tension-easers, a tall one and a short one. You can't go home empty-handed.

The short one was wearing a completely transparent blouse. When our plane from New York landed in Pitts- who was 9; and Franklin, who was 6— and they'd waited a long time before they'd decided to try once more for a boy. I wore my hair shorter then.

My father and my high school football coach, Larry Bruno, who was the chairman of "Joe Namath Day," shared the limousine I rode in. It was a nice limousine, and the boy who was driving, an end on the high school team in 1968, told me his father owned it. I was a little surprised. Beaver Falls isn't a very wealthy town, and not too many people drugstore where my mother works as a saleslady. She works now because she wants to; she used to work because she had to.

When I was growing up, my mother was a maid up in Patterson Heights, the fancy section of Beaver Falls. At night, she'd stay up late, cutting down my brothers' old baseball and football uniforms to fit me. Now my mother lives up in Patterson Heights.

We crossed a bridge over the Beaver River, separating New Brighton and Beaver Falls. From the limousine, we

---

Joe Namath was an athlete. In fact, he was a three-sport athlete in high school and he had turned down offers from multiple MLB teams in order to take a scholarship from Coach Bear Bryant.

He played before Kenny Stabler but they got to know each other. Namath led the Tide to a 9-1 record in the 1962 regular season, including the fourth consecutive shutout of Auburn in the Iron Bowl. Namath was responsible for three touchdowns against Auburn. Alabama went on to beat Oklahoma in the Orange Bowl.

Namath started the first ten games of the 1963 season, leading Alabama to an 8-2 record. He was suspended for the last two games of the season and did not play against Miami or in the Sugar Bowl against Ole Miss. He violated a "Bear Rule," and the Bear was unforgiving about his rules until you did the punishment.

In spite of a nagging knee injury, Namath came back after sitting out the end of 1963 and was the star of the 1964 national championship team. He was an all-SEC and an all-American selection in 1964. He is quite an athlete and quite a great guy.

The New York Jets selected Joe Namath with the first overall pick in the 1964 AFL Draft. In 1969, Joe Namath and the Jets won Super Bowl III, making Namath the first quarterback to start in and win a national championship in college and at the professional level.

Namath's going to the Jets is also how Alabama ended up adopting houndstooth. New York Jets owner Sonny Werblin gave Bear Bryant his first houndstooth hat as a thank you for suggesting that the Jets draft Namath.

Namath, whose flashy style in the 1960's and 1970's led to his nickname, "Broadway Joe," is perhaps best recognized as the quarterback of the New York Jets, who upset the Baltimore Colts in Super Bowl III. He attracted national attention before the game when he guaranteed that his team would win.

Joe Namath was the original celebrity quarterback. He appeared in print advertisements and TV shows. When ABC first broadcasted Monday Night Football in 1970, they deliberately showcased Joe Namath's Jets.

In 1981, Joe Namath was inducted into the Alabama Sports Hall of Fame. He is a member of the 1985 NFL Hall of Fame class.

In 1985, Mr. Namath chose his High School Football Coach Lawrence F. Bruno Sr, his friend who he respected deeply, a long-time high school and college football coach, to present him when he was enshrined in the Pro Football Hall of Fame in Canton, Ohio.

In August 2012, Joe Namath again returned to Beaver Falls to celebrate his old coach who had passed away in 2010. The town festivities surrounded the opening of a Hall of Achievement Sports Museum in the Carnegie Free Library of Beaver Falls in a series of events to mark the occasion. The events included six inductees -- including a father and his son, and a team -- into the second class of a Circle of Achievement. Every year the Larry Bruno Foundation will add to displays.

Larry Bruno Foundation board members Ken Thomas, left, and Ed Derose, above, discuss logistics for this big event. They had full confidence Joe Namath would be with them that night and he was. Look at who is peeking over their shoulder as they plan this heartwarming event. Broadway Joe may have a lot of flash but he also has a lot of heart. They sure love him in Beaver Falls, PA.

Riley Smith

<<< Riley Smith was a great Alabama QB who played from 1933-1935. He made consensus All-America in 1935. In the same year, he won the prestigious Jacobs Trophy, given annually to the SEC's best blocker. Smith's best performance is remembered from the 1935 Tennessee game when he scored two touchdowns and helped lead the Tide to a 25-0 win.

Smith was a very versatile athlete who also played

fullback on the 1934 national championship team. He was named to the second team on the all-time Alabama squad picked in 1943.

Riley Smith was born in Greenwood, Mississippi in 1911. He played high school football for Greenwood High School, and after a family move to Columbus, Mississippi . he played ball at Columbus High School.

Smith was a quarterback who could play anywhere. He was passer and runner, but he could also block, punt, kick extra points and boot field goals. He was part of the team in 1935 that won the Rose Bowl. Smith played in the East-West Shrine Game and the College All-Star Game.

He continued his career in the pros after the first ever 1936 NFL Draft. He was picked after Heisman winner Jay Berwanger. In 1936 and 1937 he missed only three minutes in 26 Redskin games, but an injury ended his playing career early.

He loved football so after retiring from the Pros, Smith became a football coach at Washington and Lee University. He became an assistant coach in 1939 and head coach 1940-42. He then served in the Navy as Lieutenant commander from 1942 to 1945 and became a real estate developer in Mobile, Alabama.

Chapter 6 Great Alabama Receivers

Don Hutson

Long before Jerry Rice, in fact, about 50 years before Jerry, there was Don Hutson of the Alabama Crimson Tide

Yes, after Hutson, it was approximately 50 years before Jerry Rice changed the way the wide receiver position was played, Don Hutson revolutionized it first at both the collegiate and professional levels.

With deceptive speed, Hutson was considered the pioneer of modern pass patterns. He was the first to perfect the technique of catching a pass "in traffic" and made the end-around a potent weapon.

"For every pass I caught in a game, I caught a thousand in practice," Hutson once said.

Hutson played 11 years in the NFL with Green Bay, 1935-45, was All-Pro nine times, led the league in pass receptions eight times and in scoring five times, and was twice named MVP (1941-42). He finished his pro career with 488 pass receptions, more than 200 more than the next-best player in his era.

His 99 career touchdown receptions stood as an NFL record for more than four decades, and his mark of 29 points in a game has yet to be broken. But each week in the fall, we look at Nick Saban's teams and wonder when!

Don Hutson has been characterized as the first modern wide receiver. He is a native of Pine Bluff, Arkansas, and he was pleased to play his college football at Alabama from 1932-34. He and Bear Bryant both played the end position on the 1934 national championship team. Bryant had the utmost respect for Hutson.

Bryant was no slouch playing end and there are many who have the "Bear" listed in their best Alabama greatest players list. Bear took no credit in for his place on the team. Instead, he humbly referred to himself as the "other end" on the '34 team. Bear was lots more than that but Hutson was a phenomenon for the ages. They were buddies.

In spite of his success in college, Hutson was not widely sought by NFL teams. He was thought of as a little guy despite his phenomenal Alabama record. The pros thought he was too skinny and more than likely could not take the pounding meted out by the huge NFL linemen.

Coaches questioned whether Hutson could be successful at the next level. But there was one coach, legendary Packers coach Curly Lambeau (Think of Lambeau Field in Green Bay WI), who took a chance on Hutson and signed him in 1935.

Hutson quickly proved his worth. On his first play in the NFL, he snagged an 83-yard touchdown catch. That first play started him on his way to 98 more career touchdowns—best in Packers franchise history. All records are made to be broken.

Hutson was a great Pro. He was an 8-time all-Pro selection and still holds the highest TDs/quarter for a receiver. He also holds NFL records for most seasons leading the league in scoring, receiving yards, and receiving touchdowns.

Hutson is easily the greatest receiver of all time—even compared to Jerry Rice, though some may argue that point. I make no judgments here. My objective is to prove the player was *great* and they deserve to be on my list.

Hutson's greatest individual performance might have come on Oct. 7, 1945. During a 57-21 win over the Detroit Lions at State Fair Park stadium in Milwaukee, Hutson scored four touchdowns in the second quarter and added five PATs for a 29-point quarter. Hutson, however, fell short of the single-game scoring record, held by Ernie Nevers, who had 40 points (six touchdowns and four PATs) for the Chicago Cardinals against the Chicago Bears in 1929.

Don Hutson's jersey # 14 was the first retired by the Green Bay Packers. He is in the College Football Hall of Fame, the NFL Hall of Fame, and the Green Bay Packers Hall of Fame.

I love to repeat that the "other end" across the field from Don Hutson, another famous Alabama legend named Bear Bryant, of course would go on to earn most of his fame as Alabama's most legendary coach. Paul "Bear" Bryant kept defenses busy while Hutson ran wild on them. You can find Bear Bryant on many greatest players from Alabama lists. I think he would be pleased to be known as the best coach that ever lived—in all aspects of the game and life.

Ozzie Newsome

Although some consider Ozzie Newsome the best tight end in NFL history, he first was a wide receiver at Alabama.

As a four-year starter from 1974-77, he set many of the Crimson Tide reception records. Overall, he caught 102 passes for 2,070 yards, with an average gain per pass of 20.3 yards, an SEC record.

Ozzie Newsome might have had just three years on the Alabama varsity. In 1968, the NCAA allowed freshman eligibility in all sports, except football and basketball, and extended the rule to those sports effective with the 1972-73 academic year.

In the NFL, he was known as "The Wizard of Oz." Newsome played in 198 consecutive games with the Cleveland Browns and he was steady and reliable as a receiver. At one point, he caught a pass in 150 consecutive games—the second-longest streak in the NFL at the time.

Ozzie Newsome retired from Pro Football as the NFL's all-time leading tight end in receiving with 662 receptions, 7,980 yards and 47 touchdowns.

He was well decorated for his many achievements on and off the field. But, off the field it was all Ozzie, not the decorations or the fame that made him the man he is.

For example, he won the NFL Players Association's Byron "Whizzer" White award for community service in 1990, four years after being presented the Ed Block Courage Award for continuing to play in spite of injuries.

Newsome is still enjoying the game of football as the general manager of the Baltimore Ravens.

Ozzie has great pro stats but before being the pro that he is, Ozzie Newsome became a legendary SEC figure. In College, he did not necessarily have the biggest numbers, but he was one of the most impressive athletes the conference had ever seen when he arrived at Alabama.

Playing a hybrid receiver-tight end role, Newsome was one of the best big-play ends the college game had ever seen, and he had the expert blocking ability to go along with his receiving skills.

Ozzie Newsome was named the best Crimson Tide player of the 1970s. His 20.3 yards per catch stood as the best mark in SEC history for two decades after he was long gone from the conference.

As noted, Newsome went on to have a Hall of Fame career with the Cleveland Browns and he became the NFL's first black general manager with the Baltimore Ravens. Ozzie still goes to work every day as the Ravens GM. His job today is to create more potential Ozzie Newsomes. That is plural, folk—not possessive!

Julio Jones

Julio Jones (2008 – 2010), a recent "great," came to the University of Alabama in Tuscaloosa from Foley, Alabama (less than 250 miles away). In Foley, he was named a high school all-American by multiple services. Sports Illustrated ranked him the top overall recruit in the class of 2008. ESPN had him ranked #2, behind Da'Quan Bowers.

Julio immediately made his presence known at the wide receiver position. Jones was the first true freshman receiver to start in a season opener for the Crimson Tide. He then earned SEC Freshman of the Year honors. Playing on the varsity as a freshman, Jones broke Alabama freshman records for receptions, receiving yards, and receiving touchdowns. Apparently, Julio Jones was not aware that he was just a kid.

Even while battling injuries as a sophomore, Jones led all Alabama receivers for first-year starting quarterback Greg McElroy. He helped lead the Nick Saban coached team to a 14-0 run and a BCS National Championship Game.

As a junior, Julio set a single-game receiving record with 221 yards against Tennessee. He finished his career 2nd all-time in receptions and yards, and fourth in receiving touchdowns. Wow!

Jones entered the NFL Draft as a junior and was selected by the Atlanta Falcons with their sixth overall pick. After about four great years of Falcon play, Atlanta picked up the fifth-year option on his rookie contract and then signed him to a 5-year extension worth over $70 million. One might conclude that Julio Jones is one of the great ones just on that alone.

For those who want to select only the best and not just great Alabama players, it is a difficult task to choose between Amari Cooper and Julio Jones. Some say it is a bit like choosing a favorite child.

Both of these men are, without a doubt, the two best Alabama receivers in the modern era. That makes both of them *great,* which is the admissions criteria for this book. Both came to the University of Alabama in Tuscaloosa with high expectations and they more than managed to live up to them. They were both key weapons on a national championship team and / or on another team that nearly won a national championship. Great talents!

Julio Jones therefore will always be respected as a great receiver whether second best, third best, best, or he comes in someplace after Don Hutson. He was known upon arrival as a transformative player. Those who like using terms that are not familiar, might have even called Julio Jones one of Saban's first—"freak" athletes—the reat athletic recruits the fabled coach brought early to Alabama. Jones sure was a cut above the competition. Freak? Probably not!

In Saban's run-heavy, pro-style offense, Jones, nonetheless blossomed into one of the most feared downfield threats in college football. Why? It was thanks to his phenomenal athleticism and size and desire to excel. Despite opting to begin his pro-career a year early, thus playing just three seasons, with one of them limited by injuries, Jones still left Alabama as the # 2 record holder in catches and yards and fourth in touchdowns. Jones' massive Pro potential convinced the Atlanta Falcons to trade a ton of existing player assets to move up in the draft so they could select him in 2011. His career stats include 179 catches, 2653 yards, and 15 touchdowns.

Amari Cooper

Amari Cooper (2012-14) is the latest in many of Coach Sabin's unbelievably talented players on his always championship-caliber teams. He is hard to match even with the benefit of time in all of football.

Cooper was a major component of the most prolific offense in Alabama school history. it set him apart as a player from everyone else on this list according to a number of experts. Of course, my job in this expose on great Alabama players is not to pick the best. That is for you to decide. There is no question Cooper is one of the "greats!"

Regardless of how you see Amari Cooper, there is no question that in his three years, he took a sledgehammer to the Alabama record book—even records recently achieved by Julio Jones just before him. When he left Alabama for the Pros, he was the Crimson Tide's leader in just about every conceivable category. He was one of just a few Alabama players to make it to be a Heisman finalist. In fact, it was the first nomination for SEC wide receivers.

Cooper also won just the second Biletnikoff Award in conference history and fell just short of Josh Reed's single-season yardage record. He was a unanimous pick as All-American with two SEC titles and BCS championships on his resume, Cooper is one of the most decorated players in Crimson Tide history.

He was picked fourth by the Oakland Raiders in the first round of the NFL Draft in 2015. His stats are impressive for sure: 228 catches, 3,463 yards, 31 TDs.

There is so much good about Amari Cooper, we may never hear anything bad. His coach Nick Saban never ran out of good things to say about Amari Cooper during his final season at Alabama in 2014:

"Amari is not worthy of anyone comparing him to anybody else," the head coach said. "He is Amari Cooper. He has his own style. He's a very competitive guy who works really, really hard. Has really good speed getting in and out of breaks. Works hard in the game to get open. Does a good job of executing, has made a lot of really big plays for us this year.

"He's certainly been a dynamic player for our team and has made a great contribution to our season."

With 124 receptions for 1,727 yards and 16 touchdowns, Cooper set numerous single-season Crimson Tide records (many career marks as well) and put up most of his biggest numbers against some of the best pass defenses in college football.

At the end of the regular season, he had faced seven of the top 50, including two in the top 10 and three in the top 20. In those seven games, he caught 69 passes (9.9 per game) for 1,041 yards (148.7 yards) with 10 touchdowns. Cooper had three 200-yard performances.

Against the six opponents ranked in the Associated Press poll, he caught 58 passes for 756 yards and seven touchdowns, averaging 9.7 catches and 126 yards.

Consequently, as previously highlighted, Amari Cooper was the first Crimson Tide player, and just the second player in SEC history, to win the Biletnikoff Award as the nation's top receiver. That is great!

D.J. Hall

DJ Hall is the son of Dianne and Mangano Hall and he has a brother, Magic, and a sister, Monique. He was born 7-18-86. He was engaged in pre-major studies.

He went to high school at Choctawhatchee, where he played wide receiver. He was one of the three most talented Florida wide receivers inked by the Crimson Tide. The Orlando Sentinel had him listed at #44 in the State's Top 100 list. He was also a great basketball player.

In his four years at the University of Alabama , D.J. Hall (2004-2007) set a slew of receiving records. When he left school, he was the top Alabama receiver in all-time catches and receiving yards, and was the first player to record five straight 100-yard games. He was also the school's single-season receptions and yardage leader and held the single-game receptions record.

In 2006, as a junior in his last year at Alabama, pHall led the team in receiving with 57 catches for 1014 yards and five touchdowns. He led the team in catches seven times and in receiving yards eight times out of the 12 games. He scored a touchdown in each of his first three games and in five of his 10 contests. He became the first player in Alabama history to record five straight 100-yard receiving games recording 100+ yards against Arkansas, Florida, Duke, Ole Miss and Tennessee. He shattered the previous record of three straight held by Freddie Millons.

He tallied seven 100-yard games on the season to give him 10 for his career breaking Ozzie Newsome's school record of six. The seven games with 100 or more yards also broke Newsome's record of four in one season.

He also had seven kickoff returns for 139 yards with a long of 26 yards and three runs for 14 yards. He played 580 total snaps with seven games of 50 or more plays. He was named the Alabama Offensive Player of the Week following the Ole Miss game and was a special teams captain for the Florida game.

Despite his productive college career, Hall went undrafted in 2008, briefly catching an opportunity with the New York Giants and Oakland Raiders. His college career stats are impressive but most of his pro career was spent in short stints and he was plagued by nagging injuries.

David Palmer

David Palmer (1991-93): Palmer was a consensus All-American in 1993. He was a do-it-all receiver for the Crimson Tide. He could line up anywhere on the field and make plays.

He was even one of the first big-time "Wildcat" players, taking direct snaps at this time in his career. Palmer was a Heisman finalist after his monster 1993 season, after which he turned pro and was drafted in the second round.

At Alabama, the spotlight followed Palmer like his shadow. Yet, his first two seasons in the pros were somewhat quiet for the five foot eight 180-pound taller replica of Darren Sprowles. er . Though he got time in different positions at Alabama, he also returned kicks They say that for kick returners, fame comes in fleeting. When he was in his second year in the NFL for example,

Palmer, 23, led the NFL with 13.2 yards per punt return last year, highlight by a 74-yard return against Detroit on Thanksgiving Day for the first touchdown of his pro career.

In his second season he got some receiver time. He caught 12 catches for 100 yards. In '94, his rookie year, the second-round pick averaged 6.4 yards on punt returns and grabbed six receptions for 90 yards. His career Alabama stats: 102 catches, 1,611 yards, 11 TD

As a pro, Palmer was a second-round pick (40th overall) for the Minnesota Vikings in the 1994 NFL Draft. He spent seven seasons (1994-2001) in the NFL, all with the Vikings. His career highlights include leading the league in punt returns during the 1995 season. For his seven year career he returned two punts and one kickoff for touchdowns, as well as one rushing and one receiving.

Chapter 7 Great Alabama Defenders

Cornelius Bennett

Having played in the (1983-86 era), in 1986, Cornelius Bennett notched what's simply known by Alabama fans as "The Sack" against Notre Dame. This remains one of the most famous plays in Crimson Tide history.

Bennett was a three-time All-Southeastern Conference selection and two-time All-American, and he was named Defensive Player of the Game at both the 1985 Aloha Bowl and the 1986 Sun Bowl.

In his senior year, he compiled 61 tackles, 10 sacks and six forced fumbles and this all contributed to his being named a unanimous All-America. He got these honors in addition to finishing seventh in Heisman Trophy voting and receiving the Lombardi Award given to the nation's top lineman. Cornelius Bennett was a force with which to be reckoned.

For his collegiate career, Bennett tallied 287 tackles, 21.5 sacks and three fumble recoveries. He did not leave football when he left Alabama. He went on to have a great pro career playing in four consecutive Super Bowls with the Buffalo Bills (1990-93) and a fifth with the Atlanta Falcons (1998).

Bennett is the only Alabama linebacker other than Woodrow Lowe to be a three-time All-America selection, also earning SEC Player of the Year and the Lombardi Award in his final season on campus, finishing seventh in Heisman voting in 1986.

Bennett helped form the mold of the pass-rushing linebacker, finishing his career with 15.0 sacks and 19.0 tackles for loss. For his career, Bennett left school fourth on the all-time tackles list. Cornelius Bennett also had a great NFL career after being chosen with the No. 2 overall Draft pick in 1987. He played in five Super Bowls and earning three All-Pro selections.

Lee Roy Jordan

Numerous Crimson Tide players have placed high in voting for the Heisman Trophy.

One of the most impressive of these was Lee Roy Jordan's fourth-place showing in 1962 as a center and linebacker.

Jordan was one of the leaders of Paul "Bear" Bryant's first national championship in 1961, when opponents combined to score just 25 points. For his senior season, 1962, Lee Roy was a unanimous All-American selection. Alabama went 10-1 this year with a 17-0 victory over Oklahoma in the Orange Bowl, where Jordan made 30 tackles.

Bear Bryant could not say enough about his skills and determination. "He was one of the finest football players the world has ever seen," Bryant once said of Jordan. "If runners stayed between the sidelines, he tackled them. He never had a bad day; he was 100 percent every day in practice and in the games."

Jordan was great no matter where and when he played. He soon became a key part of the Doomsday Defense with the Dallas Cowboys. He was an iron man. He played 14 seasons in the NFL, became the Cowboy franchise's all-time leader in solo tackles with 743, helped lead Dallas to three Super Bowls and was twice named All-Pro.

As noted Bear Bryant considered Lee Roy Jordan a well-deserving College Football Hall of Fame member. He saw him as one of the greatest players he ever coached. Jordan played both linebacker and center. In both positions, he exceled He was one of the best two-way players in school history.

While tackles weren't recorded as a stat back in Jordan's day, he did provide anchor for some excellent defenses, including the 11-0 Alabama National Championship team in 1961 while winning two bowl MVP awards in three years.

Derrick Thomas

Derrick Thomas (1985-88) is another one of the best Alabama ever produced. I am happy to report his story is one of greatness but I regret to say it is also one of profound sadness. In greatness, Thomas registers on the top of Alabama's all-time sacks list. He has more than twice as many as the player in second place (52 to Kindal Moorehead's 25 from 1998-2002). Moreover, he is both first and second in single-season sacks with 27 in 1988 and 18 in 1987.

Unfortunately, Derrick Thomas gets little credit for these statistics—both which would be NCAA records, because the NCAA did not start collecting official defensive statistics until 2000.

He is Alabama's first winner of the Butkus Award for best linebacker in the nation. Additionally, Thomas was a unanimous All-American in 1988.

When the Kansas City Chiefs made him the fourth overall selection in the 1989 NFL draft, team president Carl Peterson called it a new "beginning" for the organization. Thomas recorded 10 sacks that initial season and was named the NFL Defensive Rookie of the Year.

For an encore, he had 20 sacks in 1990, the fifth-best season in NFL history, and set a league single-game record with seven sacks against the Seattle Seahawks.

Even though he died at the young age of 33 after a car accident, he was named an All-Pro three times and went to nine Pro Bowls. He established franchise career records for sacks (126.5), safeties (three), fumble recoveries (18) and forced fumbles (45). His 126.5 sacks is the fourth-highest total ever by a linebacker at the time of his death.

There simply was not a force like Thomas before he came through the college ranks, and there haven't been many like him since. Hard as it is to believe with all the great Alabama defenders over the years, Thomas still owns Alabama's career sacks record (52.0) by a huge margin; in fact, his total is still more than double the next name on the list.

His great numbers and records only begin to put Thomas' dominance into context. He has the two best single-game totals in Alabama history for both sacks and tackles for loss, as well as the single-season and career records for both. Thomas only became better when he made it to the NFL, dominating the league for 11 years before tragically losing his life in a car accident. Only the good die young!

William Travis "Bully" Van de Graaff

William Travis "Bully" Van de Graaff (October 25, 1895 – April 26, 1977) was a great American football player from the University of Alabama. He was also a coach, and college athletics administrator.

Bully attended Tuscaloosa High School. And then played college football at the University of Alabama, where he was selected as an All-American in 1915. He was Alabama's first All-American.

He made the Associated Press Southeast Area All-Time football team 1869-1919 era. Van de Graaff also served as the head football coach at Colorado College from 1926 to 1939, compiling a record of 49–47–6. He coached hall of famer Dutch Clark.

He died in Colorado Springs, Colorado on April 26, 1977 at the age of 81. He was the older brother of physicist Robert J. Van de Graaff, the designer of the Van de Graaff generator which produces high voltages. Bully's two older brothers, Hargrove and Adrian, were also Alabama football players.

Dont'a Hightower

Number 30, Dont'a Hightower joined the Crimson Tide out of Lewisburg, Tennessee. He played linebacker for Nick Saban from 2008 to 2011.

Hightower started in 12 games and played in all 14 as a true freshman. He played as the other inside linebacker opposite Rolando McClain. In his freshman year, his 64 tackles that year were good for fourth on a veteran team where he was one of only two true freshmen to see regular playing time.

After a wildly successful freshman year, Hightower was injured in week 4 of the 2009 and he missed the remainder of the year. After a medical redshirt, he came back in 2010 as a sophomore and replaced Rolando McClain at middle linebacker. McClain had gone to the NFL. Hightower earned second-team all-SEC honors and finished second on the team with 69 tackles.

In 2011, Hightower came back again as the middle linebacker and play caller for the defense. His defense would lead the NCAA in every major category – passing yards, rushing yards, pass efficiency, scoring defense, and total defense.

These efforts earned him consensus first-team all-American recognition. He was a finalist for the Lombardi Award, the Butkus Award, the Chuck Bednarik Award, and the Lott Trophy. He had a fine year as did the entire defense.

After winning the 2012 BCS National Championship Game, Hightower announced his intention to enter the NFL Draft. He was quickly snatched up by the New England Patriots with the 25th overall pick of the 2012 NFL Draft.

He was on the Patriots' Super Bowl XLIX Championship team. You may recall that he broke up a third down pass in the end-zone in the game's final minutes that led to the now infamous fourth-down pass (which is mainly notable because it wasn't a Marshawn Lynch run).

The Patriots then picked up the fifth year option on his rookie contract. Hightower is still doing the job as one of the top linebackers in the NFL playing for the Patriots

Bob Baumhower

Bob Baumhower played on Bear Bryant's defensive line from 1974-76. He is a native of Portsmouth, Virginia,

He earned all-conference honors in 1both 975 and 1976, and Baumhower was a two-time selection to the all-American second team.

He was taken with the 40th overall pick in the 1977 NFL Draft by the Miami Dolphins, where he played his entire career. He was a great defender and was a five-time Pro Bowl selection.

As part of the 1982 Dolphins defense, which included six starters whose last name started with the letter "B," Baumhower became known as one of the Killer Bees. In 2008, he was inducted into the Dolphins Ring of Honor.

He and fellow Killer Bee, Doug Betters were the first defensive linemen in the Dolphins Ring of Honor. Baumhower was an honorary captain for the 2014 Texas A&M at Alabama game.

I found some nice words about Bob from Alabama floklore but it is real. "All of this might come as a shock to the many Alabama students who best know Bob Baumhower as the owner of

Baumhower's restaurant near the movie theater off Skyland Blvd. All those cartoon Baumhowers has on the menu represent the real deal, kids. Although the PB& J wings sound fun I advise going with a more traditional Buffalo BBQ."

C.J. Mosley

C.J. Mosley (2010-13) is one of the best Alabama linebackers during the last three decades. He was a major force in his four years playing at Bryant-Denny Stadium in Tuscaloosa.

Mosley was so good, he was a freshman All-American in 2010. He was injured and suffered through his sophomore year. Then, he let loose. He dominated the whole SEC for his final two years. He was Alabama's team MVP and made it as a consensus All-American in 2012, when he was also a finalist for the Butkus Award.

Mosley was also a finalist for the Lombardi, Bednarik and Butkus Awards a year later as the SEC's Defensive Player of the Year and again a first-team All-American. He was a member of two national champions and finished his career third on Alabama's all-time tackles list—however they rank tackles. Mosley was chosen in the first round of the 2014 NFL draft and earned a Pro Bowl selection as a rookie with the Baltimore Ravens.

Woodrow Lowe

Woodrow Lowe (1972-75) — Lowe was the first Alabama linebacker to be named an All-American three times, achieving the feat from 1973-75.

He set the Alabama single-season tackles record in 1973 with 134, a record that still stands to this day, and left school as the Crimson Tide's all-time leading tackler (he's fourth now).

Lowe was a part of one national champion team and he helped win the SEC title all four years he was in school. He was elected to the College Football Hall of Fame in 2009.

Lowe keeps increasing his legacy. This great linebacker was recently elected as the 2016 Raycom Media Camellia Bowl Alabama Football Legend and spoke during a luncheon at the Renaissance Hotel. Lowe said he doesn't consider himself a legend, but he was honored as such anyway.

Lowe is best known for his work ethic on the field and his humility about all his football accomplishments.

Lowe's brother, Eddie, was also a former Alabama linebacker and is the current mayor of Phenix City.

Eddie said he didn't even find out about his brother's latest accolade from the man himself.

"I found out from some friends first and then I called him," Eddie said for a video displayed on Friday. "When I called him, he just kind of downplayed it. I know he's appreciative of the honor."

Lowe began playing football at the age of 10 in Phoenix City, where he said the team played only a three-game schedule.

Lowe recognized Frank Sadler, who coached him at Central-Phoenix City. He said Sadler was the man that changed his life.

This great linebacker played for the Crimson Tide from 1973-1975 and is one of only two Alabama players to become a three-time All-American.

He spent 11 seasons in the National Football League with the San Diego Chargers, playing in 162 of a possible 163 career games and recording 21 interceptions.

At the big event, he shared some stories about his college coach, Paul "Bear" Bryant. During his speech, he said that he had a "working relationship" with the Hall of Fame coach.

Lowe told the assembled crowd about the time Bryant came to his house on a recruiting visit.

"I am truly honored to receive this award," Lowe said. "I know that Coach Bryant is a legend and now you're considering me one. I pour out appreciation and thanks to everyone for all of the love, support and encouragement you gave me."

"Coach Bryant knew what hard work was and from across the tracks," Lowe said. "When he came to my house, I realized they were just checking my parents out to see what type of people they were. The first day I got to Alabama, he told me I was special."

Woodrow Lowe is special.

Chapter 8 Great Alabama Running Backs

Mark Ingram Jr.

It was only 74 years in the making, but Mark Ingram Jr. (2008-10) won Alabama's first Heisman Trophy in 2009 after helping the Crimson Tide finish the regular season undefeated on its way to the national championship. The Heisman vote for Ingram as a sophomore was regarded as the closest vote in the award's history.

While leading Alabama to an SEC championship and national title, Mark Ingram gained 1,648 rushing yards to set the Alabama single-season school record. He also tallied 1,992 all-purpose yards while scoring 20 touchdowns. He earned consensus All-American honors and the SEC Offensive Player of the Year award in the process.

He had nine 100-yard games, including a season-high and Bryant-Denny Stadium-record 246 yards against # 22 South Carolina on October 17.

In that game, Ingram handled the ball on every play during the Crimson Tide's game-clinching drive. A big weapon against Florida in the Championship were screen passes. These proved to be his Ingram's signature moments.

In a great career at Alabama, he had only one lost fumble and 1,002 yards after contact (53.7 percent). Moreover, he had 825 rushing yards and six touchdowns in Alabama's five games against Top 25 teams, averaging 165 yards per game against Virginia Tech, Mississippi, South Carolina, LSU and Florida.

In those same games, he averaged 201.1 all-purpose yards.

After an off-season knee surgery, Ingram's numbers took a dip in his junior year, but he still scored 13 rushing touchdowns, his third straight campaign with double-digit scores. In recent years Ingram still holds Alabama's rushing touchdowns record, is fourth in career rushing yards and has the third-highest yards-per-carry average among backs with at least 400 carries in school history.

The New Orleans Saints took Ingram late in the first round in 2011 after he left school a year early, and he still plays for the Saints today.

The Saints found a franchise player. Ingram is still knocking them dead and wooing the fans with his exceptional play. In the year ending game in 2016, for example, on a 38-yard rush in the fourth quarter, Ingram became the first Saint to record 1,000 yards rushing in a single season since Deuce McAllister (1,057) in 2006. He totaled 103 yards and one score on 20 carries (5.2 avg.) and added 29 yards on six catches.

For the 2016 season, Ingram finished with 205 carries for 1,043 yards (5.1 avg.) with five touchdowns, and 46 receptions for 309 yards with five touchdowns, for a career-high 10 total touchdowns. Finishing the season with 4,238 career rushing yards, Ingram surpassed Dalton Hilliard (4,164-1986-93) to move into third place in the club's all-time rushing list.

Mark Ingram is a special kind of player—a "great" Alabama football alumnus.

Derrick Henry

All of the players in this chapters are Alabama legends. Derrick Henry's legendary stature will likely only grow with time because it's going to take a while for a lot of fans to grasp what he actually did for the team in 2015. Henry played for Alabama from 2013 to 2015.

In addition to taking home Alabama's second Heisman Trophy, Henry was the first to win all three major "player of the year" awards, the Maxwell and Walter Camp being the others. He also won the Doak Walker Award for best running back. Wow! Nick Sabin sure knows how to mold great teams and great players.

To put that into perspective, consider that Mark Ingram had previously been the only Alabama player to win the Heisman; A.J.

McCarron had been the lone Maxwell winner; and no one from Alabama had ever won the Walter Camp. Trent Richardson had been the only Doak Walker winner.

As the Southeastern Conference's first 2,000-yard rusher, Henry topped Bo Jackson's numbers and broke some of Herschel Walker's longstanding single-season records, including his mark of 1,891 rushing yards on 385 carries set in 1981.

With 2,219 rushing yards in 2015, Henry smashed Alabama's single-season rushing record by 540 yards—almost 25 percent of his total—and finished as the program's all-time leading rusher. He had 3,591 career yards to top Shaun Alexander's 3,565 (1996-99).

He had 10 100-yard performances in 2015 alone, to set another school record, and his 28 rushing touchdowns shattered the previous SEC record of 23 (Tim Tebow and Tre Mason).

The last time Henry failed to score a touchdown in a college game was as a sophomore, against LSU in 2014.

Henry was drafted by Tennessee and began his rookie season as the backup running back to veteran DeMarco Murray. He wore #2 throughout training camp and in preseason he became #22 once running back Dexter McCluster was cut on September 2, 2016.

Henry started well as was expected when he got his first taste of NFL action in Tennessee's preseason opener against the San Diego Chargers. Yes, Alabama's own 2015 Heisman Trophy winner didn't disappoint the Titans or their fans at Nissan Stadium. Henry carried the ball 10 times for 74 yards and a touchdown in the second quarter of the Titans' 27-10 victory in Nashville, Tenn.

Henry made his professional regular season debut in 2016 and earned his first career start in the Titan's season opening game against the Minnesota Vikings. For the season, Henry gained 490 yards for the Titans. We'll be hearing an awful lot more about Derrick Henry as time goes by. He's one of the great ones from Alabama

Johnny Musso

Johnny Musso from Birmingham, close to Legion Field, lived less than an hour from Tuscaloosa. when he came to the University of Alabama to play running back for the Crimson Tide from 1969-71. Musso's starring role on the 1971 SEC Championship earned him SEC Player of the Year honors and made him a consensus all-American. He finished fourth in Heisman voting that year, at the time, it was the best finish by an Alabama running back. Musso was ahead of his time.

Johnny helped set the foundation for Alabama becoming the team of the 1970s with a memorable '71 campaign. He had the nickname, "The Italian Stallion." His 38 career touchdowns at the time were super statistics, only recently being surpassed. His 2,741 career rushing yards still look great in Alabama program history.

He led the SEC in yards from scrimmage in two consecutive years, as well as leading in rushing touchdowns.

He was drafted in the third round by the Chicago Bears but chose instead to play in the Canadian Football League. After three years with the CFL's BC Lions, he signed with the Bears and played for two years.

Musso is in the Alabama Sports Hall of Fame and the College Football Hall of Fame.

Musso's 574 career rushing attempts were most in Alabama history when his college career ended. He held that record for over a decade, then was in second place for another decade. He has since been passed by Shaun Alexander, Kenneth Darby, Derrick Henry and TJ Yeldon.

Before Alabama broke through with its first Heisman winner, Musso's 1971 season was one of the school's best shot at claiming the trophy. Even playing out of a Wishbone formation, Musso had a phenomenal season as a senior.

While his rushing yardage was down from his junior year (from 1,137 yards to 1,088), he doubled his touchdown production from eight to 16. As noted, Musso led the SEC in rushing in both 1970 and 1971, and in '71 took home the conference's Player of the Year award while earning All-American honors and finishing fourth in the Heisman race. He left school as Alabama's all-time rushing leader. He was quite a player. He was a great one.

Trent Richardson

5. Trent Richardson (2009-11) played at Alabama after Mark Ingram. It is always difficult to follow a Heisman winner. It is never an easy task regardless of your talent. Richardson did it however, as well as it could be done. After he backed up Mark Ingram for two years, totaling more than 1,400 yards over his first two seasons on campus, Richardson surpassed that total in his junior year alone.

In an All-American season in 2011, he piled up 1,679 yards, the highest single-season total at the time in Alabama history, and he scored 21 touchdowns, another school record, on the way to winning the Doak Walker Award and SEC Offensive Player of the Year.

Richardson left Alabama on top after Alabama beat LSU for the national title. He went on to be selected No. 3 overall in the 2012 NFL draft. He finished his career fifth all-time in rushing yards at Alabama.

Bobby Humphrey

Bobby Humphrey (1985-88) played four years at Alabama. Tide watchers know that if it were not for a foot injury that cut short Humphrey's senior season, he had a great shot at becoming Alabama's first Heisman winner.

After a strong freshman year, during which he averaged more than 5.0 yards per carry, Humphrey exploded in his sophomore and junior seasons. He went for 1,471 yards and 15 touchdowns in 1986, the third-highest rushing total in the nation, and followed that up with 1,255 yards and 11 scores in 1987, finishing 10th in Heisman voting.

Humphrey left school as Alabama's single-game, single-season and career rushing leader. Humphrey's son, Marlon, was a freshman All-American and was injured last year as a sophomore and missed half of the season. Expectations are high for the next two years for Marlon.

Shaun Alexander

Shaun Alexander (1996-99) never got to win a Heisman trophy like Mark Ingram, but he was a great back regardless. He was quite versatile and he played a stellar four-year career at AU that saw him holding a number of major school records.

He led the SEC in total touchdowns in both his junior and senior years, finishing third and first in the conference in rushing, respectively. He also led Alabama to an SEC title in 1999, finishing seventh in Heisman voting while scoring 23 touchdowns, most in the nation for 1999.

Alexander set Alabama records for touchdowns in a game (five) and season (24), rushing yards in a single game (291 yards), career rushing yards and carries in a season and in a career.

Despite all that mileage on his 5' 11" 228 pound frame, he also had an outstanding pro career spent mostly with the Seattle Seahawks. He won the 2005 MVP award while setting a league record for touchdowns in a season. Alabama sure knows how to recruit.

Chapter 9 Great Alabama Offensive Linemen

John Hannah

In his prime Sports Illustrated labeled John Hannah (Alabama 1970-72) as the "Best Offensive Lineman of All Time" In a world of accolades dominated by running backs and receivers, and even defenders, John Hannah is the only guy that many pundits would say could be rated #1 in overall talent and ability to get the job done. If his pro career could be used as a contributing factor, he might have the lock on being the # 1 player of all-time.

John Hanna was voted All-American in 1971 and a unanimous selection the following year when he also won the SEC's Jacobs Award as its best blocker, along with Lineman of the Year by the

Birmingham Quarterback Club, Atlanta Touchdown Club and Miami Touchdown Club.

The Pros were all after him. Again, with quarterbacks, running backs and receivers always being the typical first round drafts for the NFL, Hannah was the fourth overall pick in the 1973 draft. That is something.

He played his entire professional career with the New England Patriots. He was named All-Pro 10 times (1976-85) and selected for nine Pro Bowls. Other honors included being one of the few players named to an NFL All-Decade Team twice, for the 1970s and 1980s. He was also the top guard listed on the NFL 75th Anniversary All-Time Team in 1994.

Bear Bryant thought Hanna was tops. He once said of Hannah, "In over 30 years with the game, he's the finest offensive lineman I've ever been around."

You cannot say enough about the great John Hanna from Alabama. It is impossible to argue with John Hannah's merit as a player. On top of all his other honors, Hannah was also Offensive Lineman of the Year in 1978, 1979, 1980, and 1981. He is a member of the Pro-Bowl Hall of Fame, and comes in twentieth on The Sporting News' list of the 100 Greatest Football Players.

Hannah is also a member of the College Football Hall of Fame, and an SEC Champion. Obviously with such a stellar career, we could keep listing awards he received but we have already given proof of John Hannah the Great

In a tough position, Offensive Guard, Hannah was simply the best. He was an incredible and unique talent on the football field. I mean the cover of the August 3, 1981 issue of Sports Illustrated featured John Hannah, calling him the best offensive lineman of all time. In 1991, he became the first representative of the New England Patriots in the NFL Hall of Fame.

Just like Harry Gilmer the great quarterback, John Hannah isn't a slouch who could play only one position. In Hannah's case, he not only could play other spots on the line, he also played other sports.

Hannah was a wrestler and competed in the shot put and the discus throw while at Alabama.

John Hannah has shown simply by being John Hannah that he is everything that is Alabama football. No matter the task, Hannah was the best at what he did. He did his job well. Two of his brothers also played as stars at Alabama. Perhaps his biggest tribute is that he played well for Bear Bryant.

Offensive line super star John Hannah is everything that is great and bruising about Alabama Football.

Dwight Stephenson

Dwight Stephenson (1977 to 1979) was recruited out of Murfreesboro, North Carolina by Bear Bryant to play for the Crimson Tide teams in the late 1970s. He anchored the offensive line at Center on the 1978 and 1979 national championship teams.

He has a lot of awards to his credit. For example, he won the Jacobs trophy in 1979, given to the SEC's best blocker. He was an all-American that year as well as the recipient of the Birmingham Quarterback Club's Outstanding Lineman Award.

Stephenson was drafted by the Miami Dolphins, where he played from 1980-1987. He was the anchor for that line also as the Dolphins gave up the fewest sacks in the league for an unprecedented six consecutive seasons. He was a five-time pro-bowl selection.

In 2010, he was named the recipient of the President Gerald R. Ford Leaders Award.

It's so hard to explain how good an offensive lineman is. It's especially hard at Alabama where you have so many outstanding linemen to choose from. Let's take Bear Bryant's word on this one again. Stephenson was outstanding. Bryant called Stephenson the best center he ever coached, and described him as "a man among children." I guess that means he was a great Alabama player.

There's not really a good way to calculate how many sacks were prevented by having such an outstanding special offensive lineman. You can't explain it but you do know it when you see it. With Dwight Stephenson ,there was no doubt that you could see it.

Barrett Jones

Barrett Jones, Offensive Lineman (Guard), Alabama (2008-12) was the recipient of an athletic scholarship to attend the University of Alabama. He played for coach Nick Saban's Alabama Crimson Tide football team from 2008 to 2012. He was redshirted his initial year at Alabama, Jones started all 14 games for Alabama's 2009 national championship team at right guard.

He subsequently earned Freshman All-America honors from College Football News and Phil Steele.

In his junior season, because of team needs, he switched from guard to left tackle where he started all 13 games for another Alabama national championship team.

Following his 2011 junior season, he was a first-team All-Southeastern Conference (SEC) selection, and was recognized as a unanimous first-team All-American.

He was the winner of the 2011 Outland Trophy given to the best lineman in college football. In his senior year, again because of team needs, he switched from tackle to center. He started every game at center for the team that won another National Championship in 2012.

Jones did not receive a second Outland Trophy but won the Rimington Trophy given each year to the outstanding college center becoming only the 2nd person in history to win both an Outland and a Rimington.

He is the only person to win an Outland and a Remington at two different positions or in two different years. Barrett Jones ended his Alabama career winning 3 BCS National Championships—each Championship at a different position—as an All-American guard, an All-American right tackle and an All-American center. That is quite an impressive record. It is a great record.

In the 2013 NFL Draft, Jones was selected by the St. Louis Rams in the fourth round with the 113th overall draft pick.

On September 8, 2015, Jones was signed to the Steelers' practice squad. On October 6, 2015, Jones was signed by the Chicago Bears' practice squad, following a season-ending injury to Will Montgomery. On November 30, 2015, Jones was signed by the Philadelphia Eagles from the Bears' practice squad.

On September 3, 2016, he was released. We still have hope for Barrett in the pros as he is still a young man. There is no denying his excellence(greatness) for helping the Crimson Tide win three National Championships at three different positions.

Chris Samuels

Chris Samuels (1996 -99) played for the Alabama Crimson Tide football team while he attended the University of Alabama on an athletic scholarship. He was a great offensive lineman.

As senior in 1999, for example, he was named to the All-Southeastern Conference (SEC) first team by the conference's coaches, the Associated Press, the Birmingham News and the Mobile Press Register. He was also recognized as a consensus first-team All-American.

Samuels won the prestigious Outland Trophy as the nation's best college interior lineman, and he was a semifinalist for the Lombardi Award. Samuels also won the Jacobs Blocking Trophy as the SEC's most outstanding blocker.

When you play on the offensive line, that is the best accolade you can receive. Samuels was an iron man. He started 42 straight games, from early in his 1996 freshman season until his last regular-season game as a senior, without ever yielding a sack.

Samuels did not allow a single quarterback pressure in 1999, had 91 knockdown blocks and played nearly every offensive snap during the regular season. He is responsible for opening many holes for Crimson Tide running back Shaun Alexander, who gained 1,383 yards rushing that year.

In 2016, Samuels was selected to represent the University of Alabama as part of the 2016 SEC Football Legends class. This is a collection of former football standouts who were all honored at events surrounding the SEC Football Championship Game in Atlanta in December, 2016.

Samuels was the Crimson Tide's first Outland Trophy winner and was a natural for this fine honor. He is great.

Andre Smith

Andre Smith (2006-08) attended the University of Alabama beginning in 2006. He first played for coach Mike Shula and then coach Nick Saban's Alabama Crimson Tide football teams from 2007 to 2008.

In his initial year for Mike Shula, at Alabama, he started all 13 games at left tackle, becoming only the fourth true freshman offensive lineman to start for the Crimson Tide.

Smith played at least 65 snaps in 10 of 13 games and played more than 70 snaps five times, while leading the Crimson Tide with 62 pancake blocks.

He also scored a touchdown off of a lateral in the 34–31 Independence Bowl loss against Oklahoma State.

Smith earned Freshman All-American honors by the Football Writers Association of America. In 2007, Andre Smith was a first-team All-Southeastern Conference selection, after starting every game at the left tackle position. He was named Alabama Co-Player of the Week four times during the season.

Smith was recognized as a unanimous All-American in 2008, as well as the 2008 Outland Trophy winner. He was also considered to be one of the best underclassmen for the 2009 NFL Draft. He was a first-team All-SEC selection and shared the league's Jacobs Blocking Trophy with Arkansas center Jonathan Luigs.

He led the team with 103 key knockdowns and added seven blocks downfield. He was penalized just twice and he allowed just one QB sack and six pressures on 334 pass plays.

On December 29, 2008, in an unfortunate situation, Smith was suspended from playing in the 2009 Sugar Bowl, a game Alabama lost 31–17 to the Utah Utes. The reason for the suspension was that he reportedly had dealt with an agent. A few days later, after losing his opportunity to shine and after Alabama lost without his services, Smith declared himself eligible for the 2009 NFL Draft. At the time he was considered a lock to be a Top 5 pick.

Smith was eventually drafted sixth overall by the Cincinnati Bengals. He was the first Alabama offensive lineman selected in the first round of an NFL Draft since Chris Samuels in 2000. He played with the Bengals until 2015. In 2016, he signed a lucrative contract with the Minnesota Vikings.

Best wishes for a continued career to Andre Smith, one of the great ones.

-------- end of listed players --------

As we noted in the beginning of the book/chapter, there are many more greats in Alabama football history. Those listed before this comment are certainly worthy of their "great" status at Alabama, and most of these players continued their greatness to the pros and their later lives.

There certainly are many other great Alabama players and one day, I hope to chronicle all that I can in a book just about the more than 100 specially honored members of past Alabama Crimson Tide teams. This abbreviated list that you just enjoyed was compiled by examining the work of many journalists and pundits who have offered their opinions about Alabama's great ones over the years.

Alabama breeds great football players when its coaches are the best that they can be. Bear Bryant and Nick Sabin certainly fit that criterion.

Chapter 10 Intro to 2016 Alabama Football Season & the CFP Championship Game

Nick Saban Coach #30

The 2016 Alabama Crimson Tide football team played its 122nd overall and 83rd season as a member of the Southeastern Conference (SEC) of NCAA Division I-A football, and its 25th season in the SEC Western Division. The team was led by head coach Nick Saban in his tenth year. All Alabama home games are played at Bryant-Denny Stadium on the UA campus in Tuscaloosa, Alabama.

AU finished the season with a record of 14 wins and 1 loss (14-1) overall, 8-0 in the SEC), as SEC champions and as a 2nd place finish in the national champions CFP series they were defeated by Clemson L (31-35) in the College Football Playoff (CFP) National Championship Game. Alabama was trying for its 10th Associated Press (AP) national title. Next year for sure!

The part of the season about which all fans have the most interest is the January 9 CFP Championship in which Alabama did us all proud, though losing to a Clemson team that was preparing for Alabama for many years. Before we get into the great Alabama players. Let's take a look at this great game in recap form.

In this way, we all get a current but lasting perspective of the 2016 team and this effort. We have already walked through the heritage of this team in the form of the prior chapters about many of the Alabama greats who were stars at different positions. They all helped put our team, Alabama on the map and these great players and others kept the Crimson Tide there for so long that the program is now almost as awesome as the map itself. Here we go with the National Championship recap. You can take it from there.

Post-Game – 2017 CFP Championship Game – The Full Recap

Uncommitted football fans across the world enjoyed one of the best football games of all-time on Monday evening January 9, 2017 from 8:00PM to way past bedtime at 12:25 AM. For the committed Clemson fans the victory was sweet after waiting a year for a rematch. For the committed Crimson Tide fans, the loss was simply heartbreaking.

In this game, the song lyrics, *what a difference a day makes* took a back seat to *what a difference a few seconds make*. The Crimson Tide came literally one second away from a repeat title. With Alabama holding a three-point lead after rolling down the field and scoring on a Jalen Hurts' 30-yard touchdown run with just 2:01 remaining, Clemson took the second-last kickoff of the game and refused to be stopped.

Deshaun Watson was the game's super-hero. However, Watson had to perform all night to get the win and he had the ball in his hand as the game ended after a Clemson onside kick was recovered by Clemson with one second still on the clock.

Just before that, without his two-yard TD pass with 1-second left, the super-hero acclaim would have gone to the Alabama defense. The big guys from the Crimson Tide spent the night chasing Watson, keeping the talented QB from overcoming Alabama's early lead.

But, not this time. Not this game. Clemson would not be denied and the Tigers had both the talent and the luck, and some might even say, even the officials on their side. Clemson's heralded QB, and the best QB in the nation per his coach Dabo Swinney calmly led his team to victory and to him goes the credit as game super-hero.

This QB, who is also a two-time Heisman Trophy finalist, performed flawlessly on this all-important drive down the field. Watson was the master on the field and the results have already made the history books. Clemson won by four. They are the National Champions.

DeShaun Watson, interviewed after the game told reporters that his message to his teammates on the drive was to stay calm; don't get nervous; and they would prevail. They did.

Watson guided the Clemson Tigers 68 yards in nine plays, completing a 24-yard pass to Mike Williams to Alabama's 39-yard line and a 17-yard pass to tight end Jordan Leggett that gave Clemson a first-and-goal at the 9. The Tigers got to the 2 when Alabama cornerback Anthony Averett was flagged for pass interference in the end zone.

"Everything was calm, and nobody panicked," Watson said. "I walked up to my offensive line and my receivers, and I said, 'Let's be legendary.' God put us here for a reason."

Coach Swinney offered: "He didn't lose out on the Heisman. The Heisman lost out on him."

From the two yard line, with about 6 seconds left, Alabama was either going to be playing in OT with a field goal if Clemson's next play did not work; or time would run out by mistake; or of course option 3 was that the play would result in a touchdown.

Much to Alabama's chagrin, option 3 was operative. When Alabama double-teamed 6' 3" Mike Williams on the left side, Clemson decided to go right against man to man coverage. They executed a clearly designed pick play, that even Watson admitted after the game was by design.

It was no accident and Alabama fans are still wondering where the pass-interference call v Clemson when on the prior play, Alabama had gotten flagged for a similar violation.

Regardless, the referees did not call it. On the play, Deshaun Watson's rolled right and threw a perfect 2-yard touchdown pass to Hunter Renfrow with just 1 second remaining.

This gave Clemson their wild 35-31 win over Alabama in the College Football Playoff national championship game. Clemson fans were ecstatic as they felt they should have won the marbles one year earlier. Alabama fans are not whiners or poor sports but are in fact generally heartsick.

They know their star back Bo Scarbrough was out of the game after a half due to injury and they know there was the matter of those two picks, perhaps even legal picks but maybe not--that became touchdowns and there was no flag. Many fans that understand how a pick play works wonder how it could be used twice by Clemson with neither resulting in a penalty call. Bad luck?

It was not once in the fourth quarter, but twice that Clemson took the lead by completing passes at the goal line on what's best known as a pick play (although coaches call it a "rub"). The final pick play was on the winning throw from Deshaun Watson to Hunter Renfrow.

The play, which is clearly borrowed from the basketball court, is simple to execute and simple to spot. One receiver runs a route that might "accidentally" impede a defender from following a second receiver on his route. By "taking out" the defended, the receiver is sprung open for a quarterback to deliver what in most cases can develop into an easy toss to an un-defended receiver.

Often, officials will throw a flag for this is offensive pass interference when it happens and the official is inclined to find the flag. In 2014, Notre Dame lost in a game between top five teams due, in part, to a penalty on a play that was almost identical to the one that gave Clemson its first national title since 1981. The Irish touchdown was taken off the board and they eventually lost the game.

So, where is the consistency? Ironically, on the play before the TD, Alabama was penalized pass interference so we know the rationale for a no-call was not that there were no flags available in any of the officials' pockets.

Studying the rules, we know that it is a pure judgment call by the referees that is not reviewable, just like holding or defensive pass interference. One would think that at the worst, the referees would have gone one way one time and the other way the next time. In this game, both calls were given to Clemson. Just asking: Is that fair? Let's say I am asking both as an Alabama fan and a pundit. I am not whining. I am asking though!

Sure, Alabama could have played better. Sometimes it grated me that their offensive performance could not have been like the days when AJ McCarron was the Tide field general. Their offense was sluggish and they depended on their defense after Bo Scarbrough was no longer on the field. Derrick Henry made the difference in the 2016 game and he or a health Bo Scarbrough would have made a difference on January 9 also.

Of course, when the stripe officials suit up in the same colors as the opponents, that often takes away a lot of great defensive actions, no matter how good the defensive unit may be playing. Making the game something that it was not however, cannot bring Alabama a W no matter their effort. Like all fans, the loss set me back and it will take a few days to get the shock out of our systems. we can

There were a lot of ups and downs in the game, especially at the end. Alabama quarterback Jalen Hurts had just given the Crimson Tide a 31-28 lead on his 30-yard scramble with 2:01 remaining. This had countered Wayne Gallman's 1-yard touchdown run with 4:38 remaining that had put the Tigers up 28-24. Two minutes is an awful long time and Watson engineered a drive that used it all up right to the last second before he passed for the score.

Last year Watson threw for almost 500 yards and this year, the Crimson Tide managed him better; but he still stole 420 yards on 36-of-56 passing and three touchdowns. Renfrow caught ten of his passes for 92 yards and two touchdowns and big 6'3" leaping Mike Williams adding eight receptions for 94 yards and one score.

Clemson packed in 511 total yards to 376 by Alabama and the Tigers posted a 31-16 edge in first downs. Alabama's bright side in the game was not its offensive production and because of that, its D had little time to rest.

Clemson ran 99 plays. All season long it was only Arkansas W (49-30) that hat had anything close to that (84 plays). Though in great shape, the D was not as well backed up as the 2016 team. Some say that this huge number of plays helped wear down the mighty Tide defense with tempo and consistent movement on offense.

Alabama did not get much rest as the offense ran just 66 plays. Its defensive depth was not at the same level as the 2015 team. The wear of those extra plays on the Alabama defense was evident in the second half. Clemson visited the red zone four times and they scored four times. Alabama had typically rejected opponents on two of every three red zone attempts. On the field fatigue, surely was a factor though there are no real excuses.

Nick Saban's Crimson Tide were clearly denied a fifth national championship in eight seasons under coach Nick Saban. The Tide managed just 131 passing yards, as Hurts had a tough night going 3-of-31.

Nick Saban saw it as it was. "They made the plays and we didn't," Saban said. "We could have done some things better, but I'm proud of the way our guys competed."

Without Bo Scarbrough's first down production, Alabama struggled for most of the second half offensively but the Tide did take a 24-14 lead on a 68-yard touchdown pass from Hurts to O.J. Howard with 1:53 remaining in the third quarter. Clemson fans quickly remembered Howard as the MVP of last year's title game with 208 yards on five receptions. Alabama had faked the look of a quick screen before Howard raced behind a confused Clemson secondary for the catch. And the TD.

It is significant that the Crimson Tide played almost the last 20 minutes without tailback Bo Scarbrough, who was injured after he had amassing 93 yards on 16 carries.

"Not to have him was probably a little bit of a disadvantage for us," Saban gave it a positive slant when he said. "I was pleased with our other backs who had an opportunity in this game, Josh Jacobs and Damien Harris, but we always miss a guy who's Bo Scarbrough's size when we want to run the ball and take some time off the clock."

Alabama had to punt after a three-and-out on the night's opening possession. Clemson on its first drive then moved across midfield before they were stuffed by Tony Brown on a fourth down and 1 try on a pitch to Gallman. Alabama then took over on their own 41.

Bama got going on their second possession on a 20-yard scramble by Hurts down the right sideline to the Clemson 39-yard line and grabbed a 7-0 lead at the 9:23 mark of the first quarter on Bo Scarbrough's 25-yard scamper around left end.

Watson was a bit shaky at first but calmed down as the O-line settled down. He fumbled a low shotgun snap late in the first quarter. Alabama outside linebacker Ryan Anderson recovered the fumble at Clemson's 35-yard line, Mistakes stopped an Alabama advance. There was a false start on Cam Robinson and a 2-yard loss by Scarbrough and the Tide was forced to punt.

When they got the ball back, ArDarius Stewart started Alabama's second touchdown drive with a 25-yard run to Clemson's 49-yard line early in the second quarter. From here, Scarbrough broke loose moments later from 37 yards out to make it 14-0.

The Alabama fans and the Clemson fans had a feeling that Alabama was on the verge of breaking things open until Tigers receiver Deon Cain took a short Watson pass and weaved 43 yards to Alabama's 39. It was the juice Clemson needed to convince them they "could." It was a major momentum shift.

Watson was energized and calm by then. He completed a third-and-10 pass for Leggett for 26 yards to the Alabama 13 and ran in for an 8-yard score to pull the Tigers within 14-7 with 6:09 before halftime. That would be the end of the first-half scoring, with the Tide held the seven-point lead at the break even though they had been somewhat outgained 203-183.

Alabama's Anderson struck again early in the second half, stripping Tigers tailback Gallman of the ball and returning the fumble to the Clemson 16. For whatever reason Alabama, just as it had done after Anderson's first fumble recovery, could not move the ball and had to settle for a 27-yard Adam Griffith field goal for a 17-7 lead.

Clemson was no longer intimidated to say the least. They reduced the lead to 17-14 with 7:10 left in the third quarter on a 24-yard touchdown pass from Watson to Renfrow. After a Tide, TD, The Tigers then pulled within 24-21 in the first minute of the fourth quarter on a 4-yard touchdown pass from Watson to Williams.

Clemson coach Dabo Swinney is one of Alabama's own. Swinney became just the second person to have won an Associated Press national championship as a player and coach. Swinney was a wide receiver on Gene Stallings' 1992 Alabama team that won the AP national championship and now he has coached Clemson to a national title over his alma mater Crimson Tide. Swinney still has a lot of love for Alabama and its supporters. He is a good guy

Coach Dabo Swinney was all emotion as he described the victory for Clemson: "This has been the most incredible team I've ever been around," Swinney said. "You saw their heart, and it's been there all year."

It was a big loss for Nick Saban. It was his first ever in a championship game. in six tries. Afterwards, speaking with ESPN's Tom Rinaldi, he was very gracious in defeat. Saban praised his team for all it accomplished in 2016, while also congratulating Dabo Swinney and Clemson on the victory.

Speaking for myself and millions of others, it was also a big loss for Alabama fans. There will be no brooding or whining, however, as there is next season and more as Alabama goes for its seventeenth National Championship. The fans, the team, the coach, and the University will al dust ourselves off and play strong again. Watch out next year folks! It will be another great Alabama Crimson Tide football year. You can take that to the bank.

Best of Alabama Football in 2016

Alex Byington of the Decatur Daily wrote a nice short article on December 23, before the Peach Bowl, about the top ten moments of the 2016 season. Alabama has already won the Peach Bowl v the Washington Huskies W (24-7). I am writing this section about some of the season's great moments right after the 2017 CFP Championship Game played last night in Florida. I expected Alabama to win and had some modifications to make to this book before I could submit it for printing.

I am not copying Mr. Byington's piece but it is good enough to copy. I would be pleased to include it as is with the addition of the Peach Bowl and the CFP Championship game, but there is a copyright caveat in the article and I do not have time to get permission. Therefore, I am simply using Alex's piece as a reference point for some facts in my list of great 2016/2017 acheivements.

Additionally, I have a lot of other notions that are not in Mr. Byington's piece that I share below:.

Here is my list of twelve great moments in the 2016 / 2017 season.

1. 14 wins – Great achievement for a Div I team
2. One-loss Season. 14-1 is a great season.
3. Played in the 2017 College Football Playoff Championship
4. Peach Bowl Victory
5. Won SEC Championship dominating Florida
6. Won the Ole Miss Closest Game Away W (48-43)
7. Won LSU Game 2nd Closest Game Away W (10-0)
8. Won Arkansas Game 2nd Closest Game Away W (49-30)
9. Won Tennessee Rivalry W (49-10)
10. Won the Iron Bowl v Auburn W (30-12)
11. Won all other regular season games by at least 28 points
12. Fourteen non-offensive touchdowns

Some Alabama School Records

More than likely, by the time these early 2016 record statistics hit the press, the records below will already be broken. Nonetheless, if you've been paying attention to many of the stats we have fired off in this chapter, this will help put them all in perspective:

Alabama career rushing record

3,591: Derrick Henry (2013-15)

3,565: Shaun Alexander (1996-99)

3,420: Bobby Humphrey (1985-88)

3,324: Kenneth Darby (2003-06)

3,322: T.J. Yeldon (2012-14)

3,261: Mark Ingram (2008-10)

3,130: Trent Richardson (2009-11)

Other records broken:

- 10 games of 100-plus yards broke Mark Ingram's mark of nine in 2009.
- 16th career 100-yard game broke a record shared by Alexander, Bobby Humphrey, and T.J. Yeldon.
- 20 consecutive games with a touchdown extended his school record.

Just like it would take a huge book to list all of the great players in Alabama history, it would also take a book of huge size to capture all of the school records held by these great players. The list above is minimal (though fun to read) compared to the Alabama record book.

I have good news for Alabama Fans. The Alabama record book is available free on line. You can read it on your PC or your phone. Here is the link.

http://www.rolltide.com/sports/2016/6/10/sports-m-footbl-spec-rel-record-book-html.aspx

Thank you so much for taking the time off your busy schedule to read about the greatest football legacy of all time – The Alabama Crimson Tide! I don't think that any team can ever exceed the record of the University of Alabama Crimson Tide Football Team. Amen!

Other books by Brian Kelly: (amazon.com, and Kindle)

Great Players in Alabama Football From Quarterbacks to offensive Linemen – the Greats!

Great Moments in Alabama Football AU Football from the start. This is the book.

Great Moments in Penn State Football PSU football from the start--games, coaches, players, etc.

Great Moments in Notre Dame Football ND Football from the start--games, coaches, players

Four Dollars & Sixty-Two Cents—A Christmas Story That Will Warm Your Heart!

My Red Hat Keeps Me on The Ground. Darraggh's Red Hat is really Magical

Seniors, Social Security & the Minimum Wage. Things seniors need to know.

How to Write Your First Book and Publish It with CreateSpace

The US Immigration Fix--It's all in here. Finally, an answer.

I had a Dream IBM Could be #1 Again The title is self-explanatory

WineDiets.Com Presents The Wine Diet Learn how to lose weight while having fun.

Wilkes-Barre, PA; Return to Glory Wilkes-Barre City's return to glory

Geoffrey Parsons' Epoch... The Land of Fair Play Better than the original.

The Bill of Rights 4 Dummmies! This is the best book to learn about your rights.

Sol Bloom's Epoch …Story of the Constitution The best book to learn the Constitution

America 4 Dummmies! All Americans should read to learn about this great country.

The Electoral College 4 Dummmies! How does it really work?

The All-Everything Machine Story about IBM's finest computer server.

Brian has written 98 books. Others can be found at amazon.com/author/brianwkelly

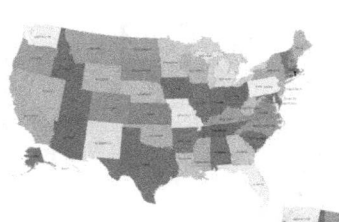

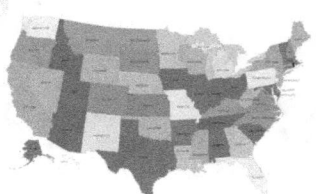

www.ingramcontent.com/pod-product-compliance
Lightning Source LLC
LaVergne TN
LVHW051604070426
835507LV00021B/2760